WHY
PROPERTY
WORKS

UNLOCKS THE
SECRETS TO
SUCCESSFUL
PROPERTY
INVESTING

Hazel de Kloe

Published by:
The Wealth Network Ltd.
P O Box28
Newent
GL18 1WG.
United Kingdom
www.the-wealth-network.com/publishing

Acknowledgements

I have been inspired and helped by so many people in my life, a list far too long to mention here - for this I am truly gratefully. I would, however, like to give special thanks to all the people who support me in what I do and who have encouraged (and nudged me along on occasions!) to write this book. In particular the people who reviewed and made comments on my early manuscript: Sarah Man, Jamie Wright, Cheryl Wiltshire, William Paice, Julie Massey, Amanda Thomas and Annette Stein.

Without the backing of some of the closest people in my life, none of this would've been possible. My parents Rosemary and Roger, my business partner Andy, and of course the amazing patience from my husband, Dennis and son, Toby. Thank you.

Contents

Foreword

IF YOU'RE SERIOUS ABOUT GETTING involved in property or building your existing property portfolio in the best way possible, this book really is a must-read.

Hazel covers so many important aspects of what you and I need consider when building a property business – and, perhaps more importantly how to do it properly.

She reveals some of the closely-guarded secrets of the property industry and helps you to come to your own best conclusions rather than be caught up in the 'hype' which so often comes with the territory of creating wealth from property.

This is such a refreshing change. Any 'teacher' worthy of the name knows the pupil must be given information and space to find their own answers. Only then does real learning occur.

With the extensive experience of building her own property portfolio and that of working with well over a hundred personal clients over the years, Hazel highlights the highs and lows of working with property and how to navigate yourself in the safest, easiest and most profitable way you can.

If you're looking to invest in property take the time to read Hazel ideas and proven methods – it will be time well spent and could well save you a fortune too.

PETER THOMSON
"The UK's Most Prolific Information Product Creator"
www.peterthomson.com

Introduction

FIRSTLY, I'D LIKE TO SAY thank you. Thank you for taking the time to pick up this book and read it. It shows that you are obviously serious about property investment and how to do it properly. This book covers many angles of the property industry, many of which you will never have come across before. You will gain a real insight into how to know whether property is right for you, what to consider along the way as well as heaps of practical guidance and tips too. If you are approaching property from a non-business background (as many of us do), you will discover the secrets about what it *really* takes to build a successful property business.

When considering the idea of investing in property, you may have looked into how to do it, what to do and where to find out about it. You may even have started doing it but have very likely overlooked the single, most important factor in the equation: *why on earth* would you want to do it in the first place?! It may sound strange to suggest this; however, in my experience most people do not take this into consideration anywhere near seriously enough, if at all. In my opinion, this is the principal criterion which will determine whether you are successful or not, so it's absolutely worth taking into account from the off.

To explain the context of this book in the way that I would in working with any of my clients, this is not just another 'how to' of property. It will challenge you to consider the more meaningful aspects to what can be portrayed as a very 'glossy' industry. The information and ideas I express in this book are in here because I genuinely care about the outcome of your decision to invest. It is my message to you and depicts my 'take on things'. It is written from the heart and very much from a 'coaching' angle, and it is therefore designed to nurture and guide you to your own conclusions. I am here to give you my honest opinions. During the course of this book, I will often tell you what you need to hear rather than what you want to hear! You may think some of my ideas are really 'out there' or they will just 'click' with you. I am the kind of person whose role it is to help you become very clear about where you're at so that you can move smoothly into where you'd like to be. This sometimes entails 'telling you how it is'. This is often the most challenging part of what I do as well as the most rewarding. Although I am aware that you may not like or even sometimes agree with what I am saying initially, my wholehearted intention is to help you 'get clear' and actually achieve the results you seek, otherwise you could end up wasting time, money, effort and, above all, forgoing that which you originally set out to accomplish.

I have written this book as an investor for fellow investors or would-be investors with the sole intention of helping you to 'get it right!' I am known for giving a down-to-earth, honest and real perspective on things. This book will tell you a few home truths about the property game and that it is not all 'sweetness and light' as many property 'gurus' would have you believe. It is an honest account of what it is *really* like to step into and be a part of the property investment world. You do not have to read the book cover-to-cover or in order; it is meant to be your own to read, dip into or gain insights from about specific aspects of property investment rather than something rigid and prescriptive.

My own personal journey through the world of property investment has been more to do with learning about me than anything else. I have discovered more about me during this process than at any other time in my life so far. It has been a rollercoaster journey of experiences and emotions, and if I can help you to have a smooth, yet exhilarating and enjoyable ride, then I will have achieved my aim.

1. PROPERTY and YOU

→ How to know if property investment is right for you ←

Property and you

How to know if property investment is right for you

SITTING HERE ON A BLUSTERY yet bright summer's day in June, I cannot quite believe I am now writing this book. Through the twists and turns of the last decade or so, I would never have imagined that I would have so much to say or so much to share on the subject of property investment. Now, in between a full, active and wonderful life, I am ready to do so. Thank you for taking the time out of what I know is probably a very busy and hectic schedule to sit down and read what I have to say. My wish is that the ideas, thoughts and experiences in this book will help you come to your own conclusion as to whether property investment is right for you, regardless of whether you have already started on the journey or are just about to embark.

The main driver
One of the common themes and something I personally am most passionate about is to understand exactly why you are or want to be involved in the property industry. This one factor alone will determine your level of success and enjoyment of the journey. It is absolutely the main driving force behind everything you do, from getting you out of bed in the morning to negotiating

a deal to running your portfolio. If the reason you are involved is not your ultimate 'why', then distractions, complications and uphill struggles will floor you when they come along.

It keeps you going through the 'downsides' of the journey
There are many times through an investor's travels when 'stuff' happens! From personal experience, I have lost count of the number of times when something just seems to 'go wrong' and you have to go round, through or over the obstacle to get to where you want to go. I can tell you now that it is SO much easier when you know exactly WHY you are doing it, as well how you'll do it and what you're doing it for. I like to call it 'The Why Ripple Effect'. It really does help you to keep focussed and on the straight and narrow to your goals.

The Why Ripple Effect

WHY is the centre of the ripple—
THE DRIVING FORCE

HOW is the middle ripple—
THE PROCESS

WHAT is the edge of the ripple—
THE RESULT

What you're ultimately after...capture it NOW!
At the end of the day, if you do not enjoy the process of property investment, or anything for that matter, then why on earth are you doing it?! The most important thing is what is happening now and how you are feeling during the course of searching for, buying and owning property, NOT the end result. If I'd had this little piece of advice at the beginning of my journey, I would

have had a very different set of experiences. Still, I didn't and therefore this book is now in existence to help you.

I set out at the age of 29 with a dream of building a really successful property portfolio which would enable me and my partner (now husband) to become financially independent. I had started my career as a professional musician and music teacher. I studied at the Royal Academy of Music in London and graduated with a BMus Hons (Performance) degree in 1996. Two major things happened to me whilst I was there during my second year, 1994. We bought our first flat, and I had a major health challenge. Now, as a student, most people don't normally think, 'Well, let's go out and buy a property!', but that, essentially, is what we did. At the time, the place we were looking to move in to would have cost us £400 pcm to rent (pcm – per calendar month. You'll see this in every estate agent's 'to let' ad) but only £220 pcm in mortgage payments. So for my partner and me, it was a no-brainer. One of my student loans was used for the deposit (!) and my partner's annual income was exactly £11,000—just what we needed to raise a mortgage of £33,000. We bought our first flat for £35,000. At the time this purchase was going through, I had second-year exam stress as well as family 'stuff' going on, and so one afternoon, I was talking to a friend and my jaw suddenly 'popped' out of place on the right-hand side. Now, as a bassoon player (in case you don't know, this is a large woodwind instrument about five times bigger than a clarinet!), this was disastrous! I rushed down to the nearest A&E, thinking that I had dislocated it, and was told when I was finally seen after three hours to 'go home and take aspirin' as they couldn't figure out what was wrong! After a series of visits to dentists, doctors and even a cranial osteopath, it was confirmed that the cartilage had slipped out of place between my jaw and skull on that side and that I had a condition called TMJ—Temporomandibular joint disorder—which basically meant that I could no longer pursue the idea of becoming a professional, performing musician and play in an orchestra. As you can imagine, I was crushed. This was all I had ever wanted to do since the age of twelve years old.

You may well ask, 'What has all this got to do with property investment?!' The reason is simple: it gave me my first 'why'. These two events were by far the most significant drivers which led us eventually to decide to start investing. After graduating from Music College, I 'fell' into teaching. I discovered that I was rather good at it and also really enjoyed it. I also developed the skill of thinking on my feet as I literally stayed only one or two steps ahead of most of my pupils. There was not much call for bassoon teachers, so I had to turn my hand to the flute, clarinet and saxophone too, and although I knew music really well, I did *not* know how to play those instruments particularly well, hence why I stayed only a fraction ahead of my pupils! I soon realised after six months or so that I didn't want to be doing this forever—certainly not the next forty years of my life! I decided to give myself five years before changing over to 'something else', though at that point I had no idea what.

I continued on with the teaching, being stuck in little broom cupboards with only a window in the door and sometimes, if I was lucky, a skylight! I also managed to continue a certain amount of playing with a woodwind trio, which we'd formed at Music College, and enjoyed doing the occasional concert, wedding event and corporate function as well as some occasional orchestral playing.

Over the course of the next few years, I had all sorts of ideas about what I could transition over to, including interior designer, estate agent, relocation agent and I even wanted to be like 'The House Doctor'!! It slowly dawned on me that all these different ideas had a common theme...property! It was my parents who finally inspired us to 'take the plunge' into property investment. Back in 1999, they had started to invest in a couple of small properties local to them as a means to building up a pension fund. They had received a small inheritance from my grandmother, and this was enough to enable them to get going. My father's career had had to shift and changed quite dramatically in the latter years, which left him without a substantial pension to retire on. They realised that their own home had been one of the best investments they'd ever made, so they got going and started to invest. They did very well, and the market at the time really helped as well, enabling them to buy a few more properties. In 2001, they encouraged us to get involved, so we did. This was quite a landmark as it was exactly five years after graduating and I had done it—I'd found an alternative to the music profession which was exciting, different and had real potential. By this stage, we had already realised the possibilities of working in the property industry as our first flat had doubled in value, enabling us to buy a house at the tender age of 25, when most of our friends were still struggling to pay their rent each month.

How did we do this? You guessed it, we raised a deposit with my husband's student loan (he took his degree after mine), and my income of £15,000 was used to raise a mortgage! We bought a little one bedroom flat in the seaside town of Littlehampton for £46,000, and it cash flowed (after all expenses) at around £250 pcm, which we thought was pretty good! Having caught the 'bug', we tried to do our second deal the year after. I say 'tried' as we did not succeed! We went into partnership with someone and the deal fell apart, so we ended up losing out. This was one of our first major lessons—not having a proper agreement with a JV (Joint Venture) partner drawn up from the outset.

In 2003, a leaflet dropped through our door and we were invited to attend a 'property training event', which we readily went along to. I have to say, we were wowed with the information that evening and were drawn in...hook, line and sinker! Needless to say, it was a life-changing moment, and I'll give you more stories along the way of what we learnt... We started along a series of property investment training courses, which had us thinking about what else we could achieve through investing, and that's where things changed!

After riding a rollercoaster of a journey building up our portfolio to sustain our lifestyle over the course of the next few years, I was then asked in 2007 to join with the organisation that I had trained with (one of the world's largest wealth education organisations) to be a mentor to their clients. I also worked alongside one of the country's largest private landlords and Channel 4 'Secret Millionaire' as a wealth coach for his business over an eighteen-month period. This period was an incredible learning time for me, and I thoroughly enjoyed being able to help other people through what I'd achieved. It was during this time that I developed my own 'take on things' and wanted to get my message out there and do things in my own way. So I decided, in 2011, to take the plunge and set up my own business. Why Property Works™ was born, and I am pleased to say I am very happy I followed my heart and took the leap of faith to do so. As a result of developing a stable, sustainable and wealth-building property business, it has allowed my husband and me the financial freedom to enjoy spending quality time with our son from the moment he was born. Having the freedom and flexibility to create our own lives has been extremely empowering and enabled us to travel, spend more time with family and friends and of course develop our business. We continue to build our portfolio to this day with a considered approach. Working on a principle of 'slow and steady wins the race', we know we are setting up a truly financially-viable future for ourselves, our son and the people we inspire and help along the way.

Anyway, enough about me for the time being and back to you! I will go more into more detail about the 'why factor' and why I feel it is so important a little later.

Know it can happen

As well as having your 'why' in place, you have to know whole-heartedly that it can happen. If you do not believe it is possible, even in the smallest of ways, then it just won't. You have to be clear about your decision and really search hard for any doubts you may have or worries that crop up as you think about it because believe me, they will get in the way! Whilst we were training, we met a wonderful couple wanting very similar things to us. The biggest differences were their personal circumstances and their beliefs. They were both from abroad and had only a small amount in savings to work with. The very first deal they invested in, they lost ALL their money, which then brought them to a halt. As a result, their enthusiasm turned to disillusionment and their belief about what was possible vanished. They tried to keep on going and search out deals that they could work on but were consistently knocked back. They did eventually end up buying a property to live in, but even this was a lot more hassle and work than they ever anticipated and nearly broke them up. I may sound quite negative here, but it is crucial to understand that it really isn't all plain sailing and that you need firm foundations in place if you are going to succeed. Being certain about what you are doing is vital, and my intention behind this book is for you to know whether indeed property is for you by the time you've finished reading it.

Be patient; Rome wasn't built in a day!

When I first start working with people (especially when they already know something about property investment and have maybe been on a few courses), it seems that they want everything to happen 'NOW'! I remember feeling that way myself when I first began, so I know exactly where they're coming from. If you feel a sense of urgency around getting on with it, just remember this quote from Joseph Licklider: 'People tend to overestimate what can be done in one year and to underestimate what can be done in five or ten years'. Be patient, the process of learning and getting yourself into a position to invest can take quite a long time, let alone the actual time spent finding the right investments and building the business, so take it easy on yourself and just do it one step at a time; you'll get there! I will always remember New Year's Eve 2009 when I received a text message from a couple I had worked with a few years earlier. It read something along the lines of this, 'Happy New Year Hazel! We are now up to 10 properties with a tremendous positive cash flow and are financially independent! We just wanted to thank you so much for all your help, guidance and inspiration.' Now that's what it's all about! I thoroughly enjoy receiving positive update reports from my clients. Watching the progression and growth of their confidence, know-how and portfolios is a real motivation for me.

It's worth it!

There's no doubt. Property investment can be extremely rewarding when you are coming from the 'right place' and have a clear vision of why, how and what you want to achieve and help people along the way. If you build your property business from this perspective, you will definitely be rewarded for your efforts.

You will have a great team around you, sound investments in your portfolio, happy tenants and a fantastic income.

The objectives of property investment

One of the first things you will need to ask yourself is 'what are my investment objectives – what would I like to achieve?' This is a bit of a goal-setting exercise which allows you to explore the possibilities before getting 'stuck' in the 'how to' part. Is your aim to set up a pension fund for your retirement? Would you like an extra income to support being able to go away on family holidays or pay school fees each year, or is your plan to become financially independent? There are many different objectives and each person's requirements are totally different to another's. Each of these needs various strategies in order to achieve them.

The Benefits

The true power of investing in property is phenomenal. If done correctly, the ability to 'create' money far outstrips your earning potential. Raising money and leveraging (borrowing) money enables you to 'beat the clock' by increasing your investing power. As I mentioned already, our portfolio was only started as a means to have a pension fund, although we soon realised the possibility of creating an ongoing income from it even at a young age. This meant we could have more choice about what we did and the freedom to live the lifestyle we chose without being 'dictated to' by where we went to work, etc. Building a secure financial position helps you to get through difficult situations, such as illness, redundancy, fuel, food and utilities increases and other significant changes to the economy. If you steadily build up a portfolio of properties alongside your current career or situation, you will be safeguarding yourself as well as future generations.

Cash Flow

As with any good business, the most important factor is cash flow. I was taught early on in my investing career to 'milk the cow, not kill the cow'. This basically means that if you set up a property that brings you money in each month, keep it!! It is a true asset. If you sell, you may make a nice lump sum, but you have no further revenue from that property. Don't get me wrong, it is inevitable that you may sometimes want to sell to raise extra seed capital or modify your strategy, and so it is a good idea to have a balance between the two.

Traditionally, the UK is split into cash flow and capital growth areas. The North, Scotland and Wales are seen as 'cash flow' areas and the South as 'capital growth'. I am being very general here, and there are of course exceptions to the rule. You will find pockets of capital growth areas in many cash flow areas as well as cash flow pockets in capital areas; however, this is a good rule of thumb. It is all down to research to ascertain exactly which areas are best for which strategy. You will typically be looking for 2–3 bedroom, terraced properties in larger towns or cities, and the objective is to buy and hold them over the medium to long term. A more advanced strategy is to buy HMO (House of Multiple Occupancy) property, where you rent a property out by the room and therefore generate more income. Depending on where you buy, single-let properties will produce in the region of £100–£250 pcm, whereas the multi-let properties will be significantly higher, from £400–£1,000+ pcm, and will generally increase in value very slowly and steadily. These properties provide you with lifestyle choices. We built our portfolio to begin with by adding these smaller single-let units before progressing to the larger HMO's to generate more income. We felt we had to have a certain level of experience in order to add these into the mix.

Capital Growth

On the whole, if you buy a property in the South of England, you will be investing here for long-term capital growth. Most of the time, if you rent a property out in this area, you will be lucky if it can cover its own expenses (in some areas you will be paying money out from your pocket each month!) whilst you hold it, but the idea is that the medium to long-term values will increase significantly. If your idea is to purely build a pension portfolio and have some serious equity when you come to retire, then this is a good option. With a time span of twenty years, your property values could rise enough to enable you to sell some off and pay down the remaining mortgages on the others, leaving you with unencumbered (mortgage-free) properties from which you reap the full rental income (minus expenses). This area is also better for doing a 'flip' strategy in which you buy a property, do it up and sell it on. Beware though, this is not an 'easy' strategy and requires a lot of research and negotiation skills to set up. The reason it works better in the South is because it is a faster-moving market and there is usually more demand for properties, therefore a higher potential for resale. Both these ideas will give you larger 'chunks' of money. We used this strategy to enable us to raise much needed capital in the early days to continue with our buy and hold strategy alongside it.

Think about your personal circumstances

The number of people I have met and worked with who would like to get going to invest in property yet have been hampered by certain circumstances in their lives is significant. Just like thinking about having children, there is never really a 'right time' to invest, though you certainly can bring about more conducive circumstances to help you do the best you can. As well as becoming aware of all the elements to creating a successful property business, there is definitely a large element of just 'going for it'. I will go into this in more detail later on in the book.

Logistics

Your personal logistics have a large part to play in where you will set up your portfolio. This depends heavily on your strategy and your personal situation.

If, for example, you decide that you'd like to build a cash flow portfolio and you live in London, you will have to start looking further afield in the cash flow areas I mentioned before. You will need to travel to the area you choose on a fairly regular basis to get to know it and be in with the best chance of finding some deals. If you work full-time, then you will have to operate around what you do. When we first started, I remember doing research in the evenings (and sometimes well into the night!), setting up appointments between my music lessons and then going to viewings at the weekend—which often involved haring up and down the country like lunatics! Some people have a theory whereby they prefer to keep close to home. If you are within an hour's radius of home, you can source and manage properties a lot easier. This, however, is not particularly convenient if you want to build a cash flow portfolio unless you are thinking of more advanced strategies. One client I worked with lived in South London and wanted to invest in Huddersfield. She was a single mum with two children and did not enjoy driving! It soon became apparent to her that this was a logistical nightmare; therefore, she had to re-think her remit. On the other hand, I worked with a couple who live in North London, have no car and recently had a baby, and they started and continue to develop a portfolio in Stoke. I guess this goes to show 'where there's a will, there's a way'! If you are an experienced investor and already have a number of BTL (Buy-to-Let) properties, you could think about whether you have the right resources to set up an HMO or explore other strategic avenues and move on in this way.

Personal Circumstances

As I have just mentioned, it may be your family situation which is tricky to work around. If this is the case and you are also working full-time and living in the south of the country, you will struggle to make this work. The possibility is there to build an excellent team to help you; it is just a matter of finding them!

Your current mindset is also a massive factor in getting started as are your self-belief and confidence levels. I once worked with a lady who had divorced a couple of years before, had two grown-up children and had never had control over the finances in the relationship. When I first started working with her, she had such low self-esteem and her confidence levels were rock bottom. She was extremely nervous about going to estate agents and asking for property details to look at, let alone booking viewings, doing negotiations and structuring how the deals were going to work. Based on her circumstances, I suggested that instead of property, she may want to start by building on something she knew about, was good at and could start to bring in some much needed revenue. She heaved a big sigh of relief, and I am happy to say, she went off and started a business doing something she enjoyed! Property, in this instance, was just not right for her at that particular time.

How are your finances?

This is, of course, a massive factor in determining whether you are able to invest right now. Ask yourself these questions:

- ☐ Do I know my credit score?
- ☐ Do I have savings or equity to release in order to put down as a deposit?
- ☐ If not, do I have access to other sources of funding? (e.g., family members, friends, bank lending, etc.)
- ☐ Can I raise a mortgage in my own name?

If not, is there anyone I can team up with who can? (e.g., partner, grown-up child, family member, friend, business partner, etc.)

If you are in the fortunate position of having a decent level of savings or the potential to release funds from your existing home or other asset, as well as the ability to raise a mortgage, then you are in a very strong position indeed. If not, the power of team work in a property purchase can be extremely advantageous. If you have a small pot of money and go to other people to see if they would like to collaborate so that you can all benefit, this is called 'Joint Venturing' and is a good option to help you move forward. There is a caveat here in that you must choose your JV partners carefully, really know what you're doing, have a legal agreement drawn up to cover all eventualities and treat it like a proper business. I would definitely seek professional advice if you are thinking of doing such a deal.

Property is not for everyone

Whilst it is true to say 'yes, anyone *can* do it', this does not mean that everyone *should* do it! The game (and I do see it as a game!) of property investment really isn't for everybody. I have seen so

many people turn up and churn through sem
after conference after networking event, et
happening for them. You see, I truly believe
other industry, there are people who are absolutely in
involved in it and those who aren't. What I am saying is
just as you couldn't imagine a planet full of chefs or teachers or
doctors, there cannot be a world full of property investors! We
each have our own unique set of skills, talents and interests, and
it is quite a rarity to be aligned with buying and working with
properties. Watch out for the following signs as these may indicate that property is not for you...

The need for money

Now, the *need* for money is very different to *wanting to* make
money from property. In my experience, people who come to
property investment out of the need to make money are setting
themselves up to fail. Property is seen as the last resort in a
series of financial ventures and the answer to all their prayers.
First of all, there is immediately a feeling of desperation built in
to the search. This is a very different feeling from being excited
about going out to look for a deal and seeing how it could stack
up. The mentality behind this need is that there is 'not enough',
and subsequently, it will follow that there is a scarcity of deals.
'Where focus goes, energy flows' is a very powerful quote by
Michael Beckwith and is so true in this case. Some years ago,
I worked with a few people who fitted into this category. Don't
get me wrong, they were wonderful people and were actually
quite excited about the idea of investing in property. The thing
was that they had bought into the relative 'hype' around the
fact the property investment was 'the answer' and could make
them rich. They believed that it could happen very quickly and
without any of their own personal resources. Whilst this can be

ͻ, it is only in exceptionally rare situations where somebody ꓘas total and complete belief and prior relevant experience in another field which translates well into the property business that this can actually transpire. In the vast majority of cases, people have 'bought into the dream', and when reality kicks in, their hopes and dreams come crashing down. With this scarcity mentality, the desperation and illusory nature of their ideas of 'property is the answer' lead them to making 'bad' decisions. In turn, this can actually exacerbate their problems further and get them into deeper financial problems. Unfortunately, the people I worked with in this situation ended up having to forget about property and concentrate their efforts on something else where they could make money. More about this topic later.

Doing it because you feel you should

Whenever I hear the words 'should', 'ought' or 'could' little alarms bell start to go off!! This gives me the sign that the person I am working with hasn't necessarily got their heart in it. They may have been told to invest by someone else who thinks it's a great idea and that they ought to get involved, when actually they have no interest in property whatsoever. They may have witnessed the property market rising, seen the missed opportunities they could've taken, thought 'I should have got involved in that', decided to jump on the 'band wagon' (as a lot of people did in the Buy-to-Let boom years of the early–mid 2000's) and then got caught out because they didn't actually know what they were doing. You may have heard about people who have had their fingers burnt by buying properties from companies who promised the world with what seemed like amazing deals, only to be either completely ripped off or left standing high and dry when the bubble burst. They were then left beating themselves up because they hadn't really known what they were doing.

You may also have heard of people who have got involved in property out of feeling the fear or guilt of not having any pension provision. They suddenly panic about the fact that they are not provided for in their retirement years and end up taking hasty advice from people they think know better than them. The result is that they own a property which doesn't actually work for them in the short term and the mid-long term prospects may not be great either, therefore completely defeating the object of the exercise! Basically, any decision that you make from these feelings will inevitably end up causing you trouble, so become aware of what you're saying to yourself and choose wisely!

Just because everyone else is
This has similarities to the previous point in that you may feel driven to invest because of the 'hype' around what the market (and apparently everybody else!) is doing. More specifically here, the point I would like to make is just because someone else thinks property is a good idea, doesn't mean that you have to also. It may be that you've come across a property expert or company who is 'making it' in the property world and thought, 'Well, if they can do it, so can I!' The fact is that they may have had a totally different set of circumstances and mindset than you, and while it is always great to be and feel inspired by somebody else, you have to search within yourself as to whether you *truly* feel it is a match for you.

You might have read somewhere that investing in property is a great idea. Make sure you do your research on the article and find back-up evidence for whichever person or company is promoting it. Maybe you overheard or were involved in a 'dinner party conversation' where someone mentioned property and that 'so-and-so owns this villa and that apartment', etc. and were wowed by the thought. Quite often, we feel that we must 'keep up with the Jones's' and forget what is most important to us. At the end of the day, getting advice and seeking opinion is fine as long as it is backed up with good, honest listening to yourself as to whether the idea is right for you.

Is it a match?

Close the book and pass it on

Seriously...if you feel that right now property is not for you based on the insights and thoughts you've had so far from reading what I've said, then close the book and either put it away for another time or pass it on to someone else who you believe it may be right for.

You may just have a 'knowing' feeling that this is not quite the right time. You may still have thoughts that at some point you'd like to get involved, just not right now. Listening to your intuition is absolutely key to you finding your own path in life, and I respect people who trust in themselves enough to know what is right...and what is not right for them. If you're just not quite sure yet and you continue reading through the book, you will gain even more insights into the world of property investment and can make an even more informed decision. My intention is that, by the end of the book, you will *know* whether it is or isn't a match. Whatever you eventually decide, either just go for it or let it go. Please do not beat yourself up for making the decision not to invest right now. Simply trust that you are making the best choice for your personal life-situation right now.

Continue reading

On the other hand, if I am right in thinking that you bought this book knowing pretty well that you had a genuine interest in property and felt that now was a good time to explore further then great—read on!

You may be feeling a grounded sense of enthusiasm regarding the idea, or just totally passionate about and loving the idea of getting involved. If so, welcome to the journey! Throughout this book, I will give you objective and balanced views, will give valuable insights based on my experiences and will aim to manage your expectations in relation to what can be achieved. Deep down, I'm a great believer of anything being possible; however, it is good to know exactly what is best and possible for you right now. Are you ready? Then let's go!

YOU

THE IMPORTANCE of KNOWING YOUR 'WHY'

2.

→ Your driving force ←

The importance of knowing your why

The 'Why' Factor – your driving force

SINCE 2007, I HAVE THOROUGHLY enjoyed working with the clients I've had through the various organisations I've worked with. During the course of time, I have honed and developed my skills as a mentor and coach and always aimed to learn from every situation I came across and each person I came into contact with. I began to realise fairly early on that there were actually very few people who came through 'the doors' and actually 'made it'. I started to question the whole process and made it my mission to figure out exactly what it was that made some people more successful than others so that I could help each and every person realise their potential in their own unique way.

Essence, know, enjoy!
It was around early summer, June 2010, when I had a particular 'light bulb' moment. I remember driving over on a fresh summer's morning to meet up with the set of clients I was out with on an 'on location' mentorship when it dawned on me that the key to being successful was in capturing the *essence* of what it is

you are actually searching for right *now*, being *certain* of what you are doing and *enjoying* the ride!! If this sounds a little 'airy fairy', let me explain... When you think of your dream life, you always imagine a scenario, and a set of feelings arise. It is when you reach this point in a conversation with someone about their dreams and goals that the smile comes across their face and they visibly relax, as if a weight has been taken off their shoulders. It is always about more than just the money, free time or choices they will have; it is about this intangible element. I thought to myself, if I could help my clients capture this before they set out on their investment journey, the way will be clearer, more relaxed and enjoyable.

You'll be more 'in the zone'
Knowing your true why helps everything become more effortless. It also helps if and when obstacles present themselves to you. If you can remain in this space, you will truly be living your best life. When I discovered that my real why was to be true to myself and help others be true to themselves, thereby giving me and them peace of mind, a sense of fulfilment and being happy, it was like everything seemed to click into place. Suddenly, opportunities kept coming up. I had private clients approaching me out of the blue, and it felt like I was literally being taken care of without any effort on my part. The more I remain in this 'intangible place', the easier the flow and the happier I am.

Faster results
I strongly believe that knowing *why* you are doing something actually drives you towards that which you want faster than any goal you set. When you 'hit it right', it actually drives you! You wake up in the morning with such a sense of purpose and knowing that what you're doing is absolutely right for you. It

literally catapults you forward. As a result, the right opportunities will present themselves to you, and you will stop worrying and stressing over the little things (and big things!) that happen.

Without it, fear, frustration and procrastination can rule

Just think about it. We have all experienced periods in our lives when things have gone better than other times. As you become aware of the feelings you had around the 'easier' times, everything seemed effortless, you enjoyed yourself and life was good. As soon as you 'lose yourself' in the mix of life and 'stuff' happening, e.g., being influenced by the news, people around you and general life situations seemingly impacting you, the frustration, anxiety and fear creep in. If you don't have your 'why' to hang on to and remind yourself about (and most people don't!), it is easy to become swept away by these incidences and let yourself be ruled by life happening to you.

Stress takes over!

It is easy to see and relate to the idea that when this happens, we get stressed. In relation to property investment (and any other life situation!), this is a bad thing! We tend to become flustered and make the wrong decisions, and when you're dealing with large sums of money, this can seriously damage your bank account! If you stay in these feelings too long, panic can set in and you feel overwhelmed.

Excuses galore

The 'rabbit caught in headlights' analogy accurately describes this. If you are not feeling 100% sure about a decision, you will either make the wrong decision or you will procrastinate in some way. This could come out in a number of ways. You'll decide not to go ahead due to a lack of confidence or knowledge, you'll get stuck in panic mode or you will go into analysis paralysis. You'll say to yourself, 'When this is absolutely right and this set of factors happen, then I'll go for it!' The stark reality is that if you stay in this mode, nothing will get done. You may *think* you're being productive by making a call, doing some research or putting an offer in, but actually in this frame of mind you are just kidding yourself. The intention you put behind anything and everything you do will determine that which comes about. If your heart isn't really behind what you're doing, it won't work out.

Stopped in your tracks

When things 'go wrong' and your property investment journey just doesn't flow, it can feel like the universe is conspiring against you! It is important at these points to sit up and take notice. There are a series of exercises later on in the book which can help you if this happens, just to make sure that you are absolutely aligned with what you want to achieve.

I once worked with a guy who had been a fairly successful investor. He then embarked on a series of educational investment courses where he was shown so many different ways of doing things that he began to question what he'd done previously, to the extent that it literally stopped him in his tracks! His nature was very analytical anyway, and so when all these options came along, he didn't know where to begin and questioned what he'd done on his own prior to this time. This essentially was a good thing in some ways as it is important to review and consolidate every now and again, but he became so fixated upon getting it 'just right' from then on that it prevented him from moving forward for over two years. After I had worked with him and helped him get really clear on why he was doing this, what he wanted to achieve and what had actually been holding him back as well as many other aspects of the property business, he found and proceeded on a deal within a month and now continues to build his portfolio with ease.

There is also a tendency, in those who stop in their tracks and/or make excuses, to blame others for this happening. They either find it hard to take responsibility for the decisions they made or outright deny it had anything to do with them. In any case, it can prevent them from moving forward for a long time, if ever. The best thing is to acknowledge what has happened or face your fear and see it for what it really is, work through it and move on.

I've been there!

It's true; I can honestly say that I have experienced each of these 'demons' along the way several times over! There were times when we just came up against a brick wall every now and then. I remember in the early days of our investing path that both my husband and I hated making calls and answering the phone to people. I know it may sound silly, but whenever we had to make an important call, we used to delay and get 'busy' doing other things so that we didn't have to do it! If we expected a call from an agent, solicitor, vendor, etc., we would see who could run away from the phone fastest leaving the other one to pick up! We were not very confident in what we were doing and were afraid that this would show through to the people we perceived knew better than us—i.e., the professionals who rang. The way I got over this was to do a stint of telesales over the course of three months. I threw myself into it and learned how to deal with people properly over the phone, how to cope with rejection and grow in confidence with what I was talking about. It worked!

On another occasion, it took six months for a purchase to go through! We became so frustrated and aggravated with the whole situation that we even contemplated stopping the whole process. I got so stressed and discovered that unless I learned how to stop getting emotionally caught up during the course of events, I might as well quit! Letting go is a big lesson I learned. If a deal is meant to be, it will happen, there's no point trying to force the issue.

The biggest and scariest lesson I had to go through was when we faced a major investment disaster. We had become involved in a deal which was way above our heads at the time we invested. We had bought a 3 bedroom, 2 bathroom flat right next to the Thames Barrier in London on supposedly a 25% discount with the promise of a new DLR (Docklands Light Railway) train link and regeneration in the area, etc. The long and short of it is that the deal was not all it was cracked up to be, and after several sets of 'sharers' tenanting the property, the DLR being built but no subsequent regeneration, the property was costing us about £500 pcm to keep afloat! All this, together with the inklings of 'doom and gloom' arriving in the market, we were facing a truly scary financial situation and knew that if we didn't act quickly, it could take us under. We ended up selling the property, losing a total of £25K (I'm sure you know what the K stands for!) in the process. Now, this may not sound like a lot in the grand scheme of things, but at the time, it was a very bitter pill to swallow. Still, it is through these times that you learn the most and therefore ultimately gain the most.

These 'lessons' have actually stood us in good stead for the way we have continued to build our portfolio, and I draw upon the many experiences (both good and bad!) I have gone through to best help my clients now.

Focussing just on 'how' and 'what' will make you less successful

If you study the most successful people both in history and those who are alive today, there is actually a common ground on which they built their successes. In addition to knowing what they wanted to achieve, they first of all knew why they wanted to do it. This may or may not have been a conscious effort on their part, they just knew. For example, Martin Luther King, Gandhi, Richard Branson, Mother Teresa, etc., all had great purposes when they set out on their journeys, and they stayed single-minded in their mission to accomplish them. They may not have known exactly how they were going to achieve what they set out to do, but they all certainly had a grand purpose driving it forward.

Why I believe goal-setting alone does not work

Do not misunderstand me here. I am not in any way suggesting that having goals and dreams is not a good idea. For those of you who have been involved in the field of personal development, goal-setting is regarded very highly, and I have to agree that it certainly gives you direction. If you have no goals, you could continue to wander around aimlessly throughout life. What I am implying here is that goal-setting *alone* is not enough.

In my experience, even if you reach your goals (and I have set and reached quite a few!) after only a short time, there can still be a sense of dissatisfaction and still wanting more. If the end result is the only thing you're after, when you achieve it, after the initial rush of excitement or happiness, there is also emptiness because that goal has come and gone. There is a feeling of 'so what's next?'

You may have heard that some people actually feel that working towards a goal can be a chore and therefore may not even believe that what they have set out there is even possible. In this case, what is their driver? Only the object of their desire, and this means nothing whilst you are in the process of acquiring it. For others who have this as their main focus, it may be that they actually don't enjoy the process of acquiring the goal, and this together with the lack of purpose can be enough to distract them off course so they never reach the intended goal. I would like to argue that those who have achieved any worthwhile goal have achieved it mainly because of what it meant to them to achieve it. This was the sustaining factor as well as helping them to enjoy the process and get to the desired result—which I know to be a very satisfactory feeling, rather than being left 'empty'.

Only a small percentage actually achieves their goals

As you may or may not have heard there have been case studies on people who have actually set down written goals compared to those who haven't. I won't go into detail here as there are plenty of other books on the subject, although what I will say is that there are evidently far too few people who even think about setting a goal, let alone do anything about it. The people who 'dream' about their 'ideal life' are likely to continue dreaming and never get far or do anything about it. Those who do write their goals down will experience a certain degree of success, but those who know what their goals are and why they want to achieve them will absolutely catapult themselves towards achieving them. Why? Because the meaning behind the achievement of the goal far outweighs the actual goal itself—it is the defining factor. When people discover this, it is truly like seeing the light bulb go on!

I have been developing my coaching style over the course of the last few years, and when implementing this idea, I have witnessed this 'light bulb' effect in the clients I have worked with.

As soon as I help them shift their focus from what they *think* they want to what they *really* want, it is like a switch is flicked inside them and they know exactly where they're headed and are 'on purpose'.

Disillusionment

I have already touched on this before in this chapter. This is when someone has achieved what they set out to achieve and when they arrive there, it is not what they expected...or even wanted (take my luxury flat near the Thames example as a case in point!). I have lost count of the number of times I have met someone who has been investing for a number of years and grown a portfolio of properties only to end up hating it! They had gone into property thinking that it would end up being 'hands off' and a passive investment. Let me tell you now— even if you have the best letting agents or portfolio managers, property will never be completely hands off! They have become disillusioned with the dream of having a steady flow of passive income only to be faced with the reality of having to deal with bad tenants, maintenance issues and market changes. Don't get me wrong, property can be great fun too and very rewarding if done properly, you just have to be prepared for what you're getting into and decide exactly which roles you want to play in your business before you set off. Otherwise, your dream could turn into a nightmare!

So...what's your why?

This brings us around to the very relevant and most critical factor in the whole equation...'what's *your* why?' Think about it. Why on earth would you get involved in a business that is not particularly easy, requires a heck of a lot of money (either yours or someone else's!) and will take up your precious time and resources? It has to be worth it...surely?!

Just like the 'Why Ripple Effect' I spoke of earlier, rather than having 'what' as your focus with your goal in mind, it is about knowing why you are doing something which then acts as the real driver as to how and what you'll achieve. This method completely turns traditional coaching on its head. When this dawned on me (my light bulb moment!), it made complete sense. I realised that I did not really want the material things, it was more about the feeling I thought I would have when I got those things. Of course, my initial focus was about the dream house, the nice car, money in the bank, decent holidays, etc., etc.; however, when you start to dig deeper into the question and as your journey down this route unfolds, you realise that it's not these things which are important, it is the feelings you have about life, the people you care about, the work you do, etc. which are far more important. Every client I have worked with in this way since realising this has recognised this to be true also and has adopted it in their own lives as well to whatever degree. Certainly, it has made a big impact, and their motivation and satisfaction levels have increased dramatically. They are no longer 'chasing a dream', they are living it.

A common theme
From working with my clients to uncover their 'why', I have discovered there is a common theme that they all share and indeed, if we look closely enough, all of humanity shares if only it were acknowledged. Beneath the nuts-and-bolts of wanting to achieve any worthy goal lies a deeper purpose. At the risk of this sounding very 'touchy-feely' and clichéd, I strongly know this to be true. Every one of my clients (from every different background

you can imagine!) just genuinely wants to feel these elemen the their lives:

- ⌂ Peace of mind
- ⌂ Love
- ⌂ Fulfilment
- ⌂ Happiness/Joy
- ⌂ Showing compassion/Being able to help others

These are at the root of any supposed 'goal' in life but in the vast majority of cases are totally overlooked. People seem to forget their true motivation and instead believe it to be about the objects, money, time or freedom factors. This is where they go wrong!

It's always a feeling or experience we're after
Now, I can understand if you're wondering what all this has to do with you and property, so I must tell you that without it, you will only get so far and you will certainly experience more struggles and heartache along the way than you need to. If you are willing to look further than your original motivation behind buying this book or having the thought about property investing being just 'a good idea', then we can work out what it means to you. I heard a great saying in a film once (though I can't remember which one—sorry!), and it goes like this: 'First, there's a good reason (for doing something), then there's the *real* reason'.

Exercise – How to find your why – a brief exercise
So why don't you go ahead and write down for yourself what it would actually *mean* to you to be a successful property investor?

1. What would you like to achieve through property investing? (e.g., your initial motivation, cash flow,

pension, security, more choices in life, holidays, time freedom, etc., etc.)

2. What does this *really* mean to you to achieve? (e.g., enjoying spending time with family much more, won't have to worry about the bills, will be working towards a more secure future, experience new cultures though travel, enjoy better quality of life in general, etc., etc.)

3. How will this make you feel? (e.g., happy, content/ satisfied/fulfilled, relaxed/at peace, able to help others, deep down love and joy)

Can you see that the common denominators I have mentioned are all there? One or two may be more prominent for you than the others, but essentially we have them all to varying degrees.

It's all about NOW
You see, when we analyse it like this, we are not actually seeking something that we want in two, five or ten years down the line; we want those things now, don't we? Who doesn't want to feel happy, peaceful of mind and content in life? We, as humans, have a tendency to strive for things and think that the goal will make us feel these things, but that's *just not true*. We live in a world of illusion with everyone looking for the same answer— which only ever comes in small glimpses, if at all. I spent 17 years living in London, and it never ceased to amaze me the number of miserable faces I saw on the tube each time I travelled and how many people moaned about their lives. If you look at the places in the world where people are happiest, they aren't necessarily the richest... This goes a long way to saying that material wealth is not where it's at; the key is to BE HAPPY NOW!!! If you have ever been into the world of personal development you may have heard this message as well as the 'law of attraction',

and to me this puts it into a different context. One which brings it home and makes it more relevant for each person. If you can *truly* grasp this, the journey will be so much easier, I promise! When you are coming from this place, things just seem to 'slot into place' and 'happen themselves'! This is really what I mean by knowing your why.

3. It's **NOT** about the **MONEY**!

It's not about the money!

If you think money alone will make you happy – you're wrong!

HAVE YOU EVER BEEN TO a property or wealth-creation event of some nature or other where the speaker says 'Why are we here?' and the audience shouts out all the reasons, most of which revolve around 'the money'! As a result, unfortunately, people can become almost obsessed with going at their property businesses from this angle. This inevitably could lead to feelings of greed, wanting to cut corners to 'get there quickly' and a general sense of 'going out to see what I can get out of the world'. As I have already discussed in Chapter 2, this is just not the right approach. In my experience, if you go out in the world with this intention, it's going to come straight back at you! Of course, I do not deny that the monetary element is important to get right and to ensure the business is viable; however, it should not be the main focus of building the business.

Investing and running a property business can be stressful

My motto is now 'expect the unexpected'. You never know what is around the next corner in this line of work, no matter how experienced you are and how well you run your business. I learnt some time ago that when a deal 'falls out of bed' or you lose money when things don't go according to plan, a refurbishment isn't as you'd expected or a tenant does a disappearing act, then you have to just take it in your stride. There will be occasions where 'stuff happens' as in any business, and the more you can 'go with the flow', be grounded and less emotional, the better.

Leave emotions at the door
I remember back to when I first started investing that if the purchase took longer than I expected or the refurbishment budget went above what we'd set aside, it felt like the end of the world. I would ride a rollercoaster of emotions from one day to the next and didn't handle the negative side of things very well. I realised over time that getting frustrated and angry gets you nowhere fast, and so there was really no point in letting myself reach that stage. In fact, the more wound up you become, the worse your experience can be!

The best way to handle anything that comes along to knock you off balance is to focus on solutions. This instantly switches your thinking to a more positive frame of mind and helps you to see outside of the box you are in. There are always ways around obstacles. If you really struggle to find them, ask for help from people you trust; also be prepared to let go of a situation if nothing seems apparent at the time—it may well resolve itself.

There are plenty of rich, unhappy people
We all know these people. We read or hear about them every week (if we let ourselves). I'm sure you know certain celebrities or big business executives who, whilst having an outwardly lavish lifestyle, are actually desperately unhappy people. Their stories are in the news, or they end up writing a book about their nightmare

personal experiences. In many of these cases it has been about chasing the money or fame in order to live the dream lifestyle. When they reach the top of their game in this case, the reality is vastly different from what they had imagined. Conversely, when someone reaches the top of their game because they truly love what they do and the money and fame come as a result, they (more often than not) are fulfilled because they have followed their passion.

Money is a magnifier

I once heard this expression at a training event for coaching young people. When you look more closely at this statement, it is very true—'money is a magnifier'.

If you're generally happy, it will make you happier

If you are a very contented person, love life and enjoy yourself, then money will only go to improve your quality of life. Your happiness does not depend on you having money; therefore, you conduct yourself in a very appealing way to others. People are attracted to being with you because of your natural happy disposition. If you happen to win the lottery tomorrow, of course you'd be thrilled, although it would only add to your happy nature and you would enjoy the money. In this frame of mind, you are in a great 'space' to be creative and invest.

If you're generally miserable, it'll make you even more so!

OK, so most people fall somewhere between these two camps; however, if you generally tend to focus on the negative side of life, always commenting about how awful the weather/partner/ state of the country is, then having money will not necessarily make you happier. The initial thrill of having more money will be exciting, but when this wears off, you are left feeling worried about people trying to take it from you or what happens if you lose it in some way or the burden of responsibility is too much because you don't know how to handle it, etc. Ultimately, you will end up making 'bad' investment decisions and sabotaging yourself. Think about a time when you had a windfall and how you felt about it; this will help you understand what I mean and leads me onto the next point.

Whatever your beliefs are around money, they will manifest—watch out!

EXERCISE

How to know what you believe about money
Below is a set of questions designed to help you find out what your deep down thoughts and beliefs are about money. You may never have realised what you've really been thinking about money, so now it's time to unlock!

This exercise will help you to become aware of those beliefs you hold and if they do not serve you, enable you to work through them and let them go.

1. What did I hear about money whilst I was growing up?
2. What did my parents teach me about money?
3. What did I therefore think about money as a child?
4. Do I make money effortlessly or find it a struggle?
5. How do I feel about money now?
6. How well do I handle my finances?
7. What do I believe about those who are very wealthy?
8. Do I know and respect anyone who has money?
9. What do I believe about them?
10. Anything else?

I had a client whom I explored this subject with at length, and it helped her to realise all the negative connotations she had been holding onto about money all her life. Whilst I want you to be aware of this, I do not want you to dwell on it. Your focus and energy is to go towards that which you are most passionate about and enjoy doing. This exercise merely helps you to unblock whatever may be holding you back from doing so productively. More about the process of unblocking that which you uncover later on.

The need for money will repel it

As I mentioned earlier, the number of clients I have worked with over the years who came to me because they 'needed the money' has been staggering. Seriously, if you are coming from this point of view when setting out along this path, PLEASE DON'T DO IT!!! I mean this in the best possible way. I have witnessed too many people who have been literally 'sucked in' by the hope of fast, easy wealth creation only to end up in much more debt than when they first started.

Coming from a 'lack' mentality does not bode well

Whichever way you look at it, the 'need' for anything is actually describing a 'lack' of it. If you come to something as big as investing in property with a lack mentality, you are almost certain to be setting yourself up for failure. This is not to be confused with those who have 'made it' from nothing as these people have not been focussing on the lack of anything, but rather their love of something or their ultimate goal. Thinking that you 'don't have enough' will only attract more of what you don't have—and in this case, it's money! I can only tell this to you because I have lived through it myself and seen others go through the pain of it. I had a moment fairly early on in my investing career when my lack mentality reared its ugly head. Way back when, my first 'big hairy goal' was to own a £1M portfolio by the time I was 30. Somehow, nine days before I turned 30, we owned just over a £1M portfolio, and I was very pleased and amazed at how we had pulled it off. However, it was soon after this event that I realised that a few of the decisions we were making along the way were not all for the best... I wasn't even aware I had a lack mentality until certain decisions we made led us to a 'titanic moment' I described earlier regarding the Thames-side apartment. I knew something had gone very wrong and needed to be put right. It was in this moment that I faced my fear and was able to acknowledge the feelings I had and eventually come through it. I had actually grown up with quite a sense of lack and hadn't realised this carried through into my adult years. It is a very unpleasant feeling and is a position which no person should make decisions from! We fortunately were able to accept taking a loss on this investment to stop it from being a chain around our necks and move on in a more positive direction. Once we had let the property go, it dawned on me that we had invested in it from a place of lack (of money) and that's exactly what it had given us back!

Always look to fulfil the need first
The biggest lesson from this experience is to ensure that whatever need for money you have is plugged before you invest. This may mean increasing your income in some other way. Believe it or not, I have actually worked with people who have come to me with no job and no savings to begin investing! I have literally told them to go out and get work before they do anything else, regardless of how many wealthy friends or relatives they may have! Whatever anyone says, if you have an immediate need for money, you MUST fill this before any further course of action.

The next point to make here is to fulfil the deeper need which I have spoken of in some depth already in the 'why' chapter.

If you feel fulfilled in yourself, then investing will come much more easily to you.

The 'Rubber Ring' analogy
There is a fantastic story I once heard, which I tell most of my clients to illustrate what I mean, that goes like this...

Imagine you are out at sea and have fallen overboard. You cannot swim and are floundering around, arms flailing desperately to keep your head above the water. You are panicking and calling for help when you see someone else in the distance. They are pushing a rubber ring towards you for you to grab on to, but however hard you try to reach it, it just keeps floating away from you. This goes on until you hear them call, 'Stay still!' Because of your rising panic levels, you continue to wave and beat the water in a desperate attempt to get to the ring. 'Just stay still!' comes the voice again. This time, you listen and calm down. You stop flapping around and automatically you just tread the water. As you have ceased from creating more panic-driven outward waves from yourself, the rubber ring drifts gently towards you, and you place it over your head and are able to be brought to safety. I hope this 'rings' true!

It's always about the end result, which is a feeling or experience

When you really think about it, nothing is ever about the money. Contrary to popular belief, money on its own is *not* a motivator. Money in itself has no inherent value, so it is always about what it can buy that gives it meaning. Ask yourself this...

What does it mean to you to have the money?
This really brings us full-circle round back to the 'why'. Whatever the money can bring to you ultimately leads to a

feeling or experience you desire. For example, if you picture your dream car, the way it looks, how it is to drive and the sound it makes, what happens? A broad smile starts to emerge across your face, right?! What feelings can you imagine as you drive the car? Exhilaration, freedom, joy, excitement? What do you experience as you admire the car? A sense of satisfaction, happiness, wonder? All of these are much deeper than the superficial nature of the money which bought the car or even the car itself.

Come from the feeling or 'end result' you want to achieve—first!

It is this focus, the 'end result', that I am suggesting you concentrate on. You will soon find that the more 'in tune' you *feel* with what you desire the more things will come into your experience which make you feel that way...the rubber ring analogy in practice!

Focus on the meanings behind the monetary aspects as a priority, and the sense of fulfilment, peace, deep joy and love you are after will become an everyday experience.

My own personal experience of this was in setting up my business, Why Property Works™. I knew exactly how I wanted the business to operate, what I wanted my clients to experience and the results they would achieve; my feelings about this drove the business. The more I thought about how I could best help people and how many satisfied clients I would have, the more synchronistic events happened to bring this about. It was just like watching the pieces of a jigsaw falling into place almost by themselves! Opportunities and people presented themselves to me in very unexpected ways, which led in fact to the team of people I work very closely in conjunction with in my business now.

The same happens for my clients. When they get exceptionally clear about their end objectives, events line themselves up in their favour. One lady I met at a property networking evening immediately came up to me after I'd done a 30-second introduction and wanted to book an initial session. I was so bowled over and asked her why she had rushed up to me. Her answer was that what I had said really hit home to her. She knew she needed help, and it felt right to work with me. We met up and started working together. Within just six weeks of meeting, she acquired her first property, which would net her about £20,000 of added value (on a property worth a total of £80,000) as well as a very decent monthly income and pull most if not all her money back out so that she could do it all over again. She was very clear on her purpose, and this was a perfect place for her to invest from. She was certain of what she was doing, and the combination made a massive difference to what she achieved.

You'll enjoy yourself more and others will experience this too

The fact that I am aligned with what I want from my business, which in turn aligns with what people really want from their property investments, means that I have very happy clients! It is also a question of 'like attracts like', and I can honestly say that I have been extremely fortunate to have had such wonderful people to work with over the years. It is so true that the more you *are* how you *want to be*, the more people you will come across who share the same values as you. If you think about the friends you have, I would hazard a guess that you are friends with them because they *are like you*!! The more you can put yourself in the right 'feeling' place, not just the right 'head' place, the more of a positive impact you'll have on the people around you.

To quote the words of Bobby McFerrin, 'Don't worry, be happy!'

4. Start with the RIGHT investment

MINDSET

→ It's all in your head ←

Start with the right investment mindset

It's all in your head!

WHATEVER YOU WANT TO DO in life, it all starts with a decision made in your head. Whether it is a personal or business decision, what you choose and, more importantly, what you choose to *believe* about that decision is what really matters. In terms of investing in property, your thoughts and beliefs will play a big part in determining whether or not you will succeed.

It has to be what you really want to do

If you have chosen to walk the path of property investment, the chances are that you are someone who likes the idea, has maybe already had some experience and would like to explore the options further. We have looked at the reasons why you ultimately want to be involved, now we're looking on a more practical level.

Find the way that's right and works best for you. You may have heard about people who do everything from sourcing their own deals, project managing refurbishments or developments right through to sales and/or letting the property. On the flip side of the equation, others prefer to outsource the 'legwork' and benefit from having someone else's expertise on their side to help them build a profitable portfolio. It really is horses for courses. Essentially, what I am saying here is not to spend your life doing something that doesn't make you happy!

What you think can become your experience
By our very nature, human beings can be pretty negative a lot of the time. Translated into property, this could be disastrous if you let your mind dwell on problems or see things going wrong in your mind on a project. I have known a few 'worrywarts' in my time, and you can see where they have almost willed their problems into being by the way they think and talk a lot of the time. I know I am touching on the metaphysical here; however, I have witnessed it and even experienced it myself on one or two occasions!

So watch out! Your thoughts can have a massive impact on your experiences. There is a good side to this in that the more genuinely positive you are the better things pan out, too!

> *"If you believe you can or you believe you can't, you're right."*
> —HENRY FORD

At the end of the day, if you really want to do something and you completely believe you can, then you will.

A very interesting exercise is to become more aware of the feelings you are having in relation to all your property activities. They will give you a huge clue as to what you are thinking. The next step is to then notice the exact thoughts you are having and either reinforce them if they are positive and make you feel good, or just let them go. This happens naturally in the process of becoming more aware of them, so there is no 'hard work' to try to do this. Just remember that you will automatically self-sabotage yourself if it's not something you really want to do. Keep an eye out for procrastination, laziness and lack of enthusiasm!

If you consistently feel passionate about property and love the processes involved to greater or lesser degrees, then it's pretty safe to say you're on the right track. You will win through and achieve the success you are looking for.

A little bit of information can be a dangerous thing

With so much information and resources 'out there', particularly on the internet, it is really hard to sort out the 'wheat from the chaff' and know what is truly good information. To be able to find the best information specifically for you is almost impossible!!

You cannot truly learn property investment in a short time

Regardless of what people may tell you, you cannot condense 10, 20, or 30 years of experience into a weekend event and have someone learn from that event what to do *properly*. To become a great investor takes time, just like any other profession out there. It takes time, patience, learning and experience, just like a doctor or teacher. Of course, you must start with the first steps and put what you learn into practice. The trouble is, I have seen too many people implement incorrect strategies for their circumstances, go full tilt and put everything they own into their first investment and go about things in totally the wrong way on the strength of attending only one or two events.

You must take one step at a time, slowly and steadily, get the best education on the subject that you possibly can and put it into practice. Be patient with yourself and don't rush into anything. In taking your time during these crucial first stages of investing, you can learn how to navigate towards what is best for you and implement the right strategy to move you forward in a way that is as safe, ethical and profitable as you possibly can.

Being caught up in hype and excitement takes your feet off the ground

Many totally rational and well-educated people make crazy decisions from this frame of mind. They get carried away in the 'bubble' and whooped up by the hype, which so often surrounds the wealth-creation industry in general these days. Seeing the 'expert' up on stage or at the front of a room telling you their life story, big successes and how you can do it too is all very well and is certainly inspiring, though when reality sets in a little way down the line, you realise it is not all a bed of roses.

This can result in making decisions without thinking of the consequences. You could even end up trusting the judgement of others to know what is best for you, which puts you totally on a back foot and out of control of the situation. At this point, you no longer really know what you are doing and are letting yourself be swept along in the mix—a dangerous place to be...

You could make very costly mistakes

I have worked with several clients who have acted from this point of view and been stung, sometimes extremely badly and to the tune of their entire life savings or, worse still, put them heavily into debt which they could not afford.

To give you a couple of examples...

I was with a young man who had heard that property investment was a good idea. He had decided to take matters into his own hands and do some 'research' on the internet for companies which supplied investment properties. He came across a few and signed up to receive their property alerts. He met up with one particular company who did the typical schmoozing and being over-generous with the truth on him. He was sent through a deal which stacked up incredibly well on paper. Ten pages of pictures, numbers, location details, etc. which all looked fantastic. Unfortunately, he took them too literally at their word and ended up buying the property sight-unseen from those ten pieces of paper. I know, I can hear you cry, 'Was he MAD?!' Yes, in all reality he was. The point I am making is that he was a very well-educated person who is normally very careful with money, but sadly there are plenty of people in his situation who are duped into this type of investment. Make sure you are not one of them! By the time he came to work with me, he had also experienced a rogue letting agent who kept placing diabolical tenants in the property who either left owing him money or causing damage; a refurbishment budget which was not actually spent on the property but went into the company's coffers; an incorrect market valuation, which actually placed him in negative equity; and a deal which was structured in a less-than-legal way. All-in-all, a real mess. He still hadn't visited the place, so I made him face facts and go and see it. I helped him as best I could to sort out the predicament he was in, which at least meant he was able to let the property to cover his ongoing expenses, but at the end of it all, he was devastated and left without any money to continue with his investment objectives. A very bad experience which has left a nasty taste in his mouth in relation to property.

Another set of clients attended a couple of weekend property training events and left feeling confident to strike out on their own. They remortgaged their own home to the tune of £200K and set about investing. To cut a long story short, within six months of attending the courses they had acquired two properties needing full refurbishment in an area which was not actually going to fit their strategy or budget. These properties took up the entire amount of funding they had raised, cost them weekends and evenings of blood, sweat and tears (literally!) for incredibly small returns! They felt what they described as an 'abyss' looming in terms of how they were going to be able to move forward and called on me to help. I am pleased to say that they now have a plan to restructure what they are doing and move forward in a much more positive and constructive way.

These are to describe but a few; there are dozens more 'horror' stories I could tell, but I think you get the point!

Make sure your head, heart and gut are in alignment

When you truly listen to and act upon this point, you will find that everything just appears to slot into place. Some of the best investors and business leaders in the world operate from these principles, so why should we do any differently if we want to achieve any measure of success in our own lives? You will often find the best business leaders in the world recommend operating from this basis every time—after having digested all the 'head stuff' first. People like Richard Branson, Oprah Winfrey and even Albert Einstein are real advocates of this in their interviews and quotes. Here are some of my favourites:

> *"The only real valuable thing is intuition."*
> —ALBERT EINSTEIN

"Intuition becomes increasingly valuable in the new information society precisely because there is so much data."
—JOHN NAISBITT

"Follow your instincts. That's where true wisdom manifests itself."
—OPRAH WINFREY

"I never get the accountants in before I start up a business. It's done on gut feeling, especially if I can see they are taking the Mickey out of the consumer."
—RICHARD BRANSON

If something just doesn't 'sit' or 'feel' right—walk away

I guess this is what you would call intuition. I'm sure you are able to think of occasions in your life (whatever the circumstances) where you have experienced this and have 'just known' what is best. The opposite of this is to go against your intuition and act from an 'I know best' place in the head. This is what I described earlier in my story about the first HMO I took on, and look how that turned out! The power of this is to be taken seriously as it can help guide you through the 'noise' that is the world of property investment and keep you on your own personal track. It knows better than 'you'!

Be wary, however, of the feeling of fear. This must not be confused with a 'niggling feeling' coming from your intuitive sense. It can be misleading when you are scared to do something as opposed to knowing it is the wrong thing to do...if that makes sense! For example, the first time you buy a property, you *can* be *certain* it is the right thing to do *and also* feel afraid of the process. It is a different thing altogether to work through the fear rather than listen to your intuition. I will cover this in a later chapter.

Be certain

When your head, heart and gut 'line up' as described above, you will feel a strong sense of certainty and knowing what you are doing. This is always how I want my clients to feel when they are 'out there' in the field. It also enables you to feel confident in what you are doing, which normally overrides any feeling of fear. As I have mentioned though, it is still possible to feel nervous or fearful and yet be certain it is the right thing to do. Just like having to discipline a child for the first time, you know it is the right thing to do, yet you may feel afraid to. All I can say is that the more you do something with certainty, the lesser the fear and angst.

By learning to trust yourself, the more you will be true to yourself and only 'let in' that which is right for you to do.

When everything 'stacks up', you're there!

So, you've learned as much as you can to begin with and have started to go out and find some deals. You've found out all you can about the properties you're interested in and have researched and analysed them. You have done your calculations and made sure that the numbers are right. This equates to being a 'green light' in your head.

You're really enjoying the process and find yourself staying up late into the night to look on Rightmove and other property-related websites (this is sometimes called 'property porn'!!). You love finding out more from whichever source has led you to the prospective deal and are looking forward to the prospect of making the deal work out. This is now a 'green light' in your heart.

When you go out to view the properties and get a feel for what you're looking at, you gain more and more confidence in what you're doing. You find a property which is 'just right' and have that knowing feeling in your gut, just like maybe when you bought your own home or met your life partner and everything worked out. This, of course, is the 'green light' from your gut, which tells you to go ahead and aim to close the deal.

This is it—you've made it through the plethora of information, advice and opinion to a deal that works for YOU! Congratulations!

Get a mentor!

Whether you are new to this business or have been investing for some time, the value of having a mentor is enormous. If you think you 'know it all', then you close the door to other opportunities which may prove to be much more beneficial. I have worked with people at different stages of their investing journey and have found that we all need help to better the processes along the way. If someone has achieved what you would like to and can help you learn how to do it in a better way and the best way for you, then this is extremely powerful.

I continue to have mentors myself in my business even now. I do not profess to 'know it all'; I don't think anyone ever does. Those who claim to are kidding themselves. If we can all help each other up the next rung of the ladder, then that is a great purpose to live for.

How to choose the best one for you
When I was a mentor with the previous organisation I worked for, there were approximately a dozen mentors for people to choose from. One of the most frequently asked questions from

the people attending the events was 'How do I choose a mentor?' I would respond by saying that a lot of it has to do again with a gut feeling about someone. You will be entrusting yourself to this person for hours of work together potentially over several months, and so it is vital that you have trust in that person. It is a good idea also to check that they have worked with the strategies you wish to pursue and have achieved that which you are aiming to achieve. They have to be approachable, and you need to feel you can be honest and open with them as much as they need to be the same back. The mentoring process is very much built on these aspects. The right mentor will also tell you what you need to hear, not just what you want to hear, and will always encourage you to step up and do what's best for you.

They can save you a huge amount of time and money

I have met and worked with a number of people who have tried to 'go it alone' and have done so to varying degrees of success. After the time I have spent with them, even the ones with established portfolios have turned to me and said how much they learned from my approach and ways of doing things. I strongly believe that 'no man is an island' and the DIY approach will only get you so far. All the greatest business people in the world have always had a team of people around them to support, teach and mentor them through various processes...not one of them will have done it alone. Going it alone really is a false economy and could cost you years as well as tens if not hundreds of thousands of pounds along the way.

You may question the need for a mentor in your investment journey as it will inevitably cost money to employ their services. The greatest logic to this is that a mentor should end up saving and making you far more money in the long run if they are worth their salt. (Make sure you read thoroughly the section on due diligence around choosing people to work with later on in Chapter 6.) They have already trodden the path and know the way. I remember clearly the words 'Learning from your own mistakes is good, but if you can learn from someone else's, that's even better!'

A good one can springboard you forward years!
Having made you aware of the pitfalls you may face and best ways to avoid them, a good mentor will also help you understand which options you have in front of you. A mentor may be strong in one particular strategy and be able to tell you exactly what you'll need to do in order to implement it; however, one who has a more rounded approach will discuss with you and remain neutral and unbiased about the various options you may have. Through experience and know-how, a mentor can see things from a totally different perspective than you and can therefore help you to see things in a way that you may never have even considered on your own.

My preferred style is a combination of coaching and mentoring. I feel that the balance between helping someone come to their own conclusions through the coaching element and then working on the implementation with the mentoring aspect is by far the most powerful and ethical combination.

GOAL!

5.

How to deal with what's STOPPING you

How to deal with what's stopping you

What to do if you think the answer is 'yes' though you're still feeling unsure

OK—SO YOU'VE READ THROUGH THE first few chapters and are quite sure that property investment is (still) for you. However, there may be a small niggle that just won't quite go away in the form of a doubt or a worry. This is quite common and can come up occasionally throughout the course of your investing exploits. This chapter is designed to help you to iron out those niggles, blast them 'out of the water' and enable you to move on or to help you come to the conclusion that it may not be the right time just yet.

Go through the checklist

The first exercise is to go through a checklist to make sure that your current circumstances 'fit' with embarking on an investment journey. As a reminder, I have listed them below for you to jot a few notes down and see how they relate to you right now. Feel free to write down whatever feels relevant to mention without leaving anything out. It is important to address everything, as it may be something that you consider to be insignificant but turns out to be the stumbling block.

CHECKLIST EXERCISE:

PERSONAL CIRCUMSTANCES – What is your current career? Do you have time to work around this or will you need help?

PERSONAL CIRCUMSTANCES – Do you have a family to consider? How will it impact/affect your relationships whilst you are progressing towards building this business? How would you like to ensure you are still able to enjoy time together?

LOGISTICS – Do you live close by to where you'd like to invest or far away? How are you going to overcome any distance/travelling issues?

FINANCIAL SITUATION – Do you have access to funds in the form of cash, equity, stocks and shares, bonds, trusts, borrowed money from banks, family or friends, etc.?

MINDSET – What is your attitude to risk, starting a new enterprise, thoughts about whether you can do it or not and be successful?

Check your gut feeling
Deep down you will actually know whether property investment is right for you or not. This goes back to the idea of alignment

between what your head is thinking, what your heart tells you and what your gut 'knows' or 'feels'. I find it helpful often just to sit and contemplate and 'let the answer come to you' if you are finding it tough to decipher. If you are trying to force yourself to come to a conclusion, let it go. Remember back to the rubber ring story! The more you try to make something happen, the more you will repel it. Be aware that the answer may not come straight away, it may just dawn on you a day or two later. You are aiming to feel a 'knowing' about what is the best course of action. If you rely on just your head to make decisions, you will find that this can lead you down the garden path! I'm sure you can recall circumstances in your life where you've thought 'that's a good idea!' (without 'checking in' with yourself), and it has ended up either not working out as you'd expected, or indeed a total disaster! In any case, it is always best to take a bit of time before you embark on anything to reach this sense of alignment within yourself.

If for some unexplained reason you notice there is a 'nagging' feeling which just won't go away, you must trust yourself and listen to it. Your 'inner knowing' is often better than your mental knowing. If this happens to you and you just can't put your finger on it, then it may be telling you that it's just not right for you. There are plenty of resources in this book to help you work through this and know for sure.

If you find in the end that your gut tells you not to go for it right now, then listen! Isn't it better to be pre-warned than go down a path which may lead you to a dead-end? Remember that your gut feeling is telling you what is right for you *now* and this can change in the future. You can always come back to the idea later on down the line and 'check in' again. When you have that feeling of clarity and knowing that it is a good idea, then go for it!

Your subconscious beliefs are very powerful

Whatever you believe about will come about! I've said before that the beliefs and thoughts you have influence your experience of the world around you. I have known almost every person I have worked with to be carrying around 'baggage' in the form of beliefs which will not serve them in their quest to build and run a successful property portfolio. When I've done some digging around what may stop them in their quest, I get to their root negative belief, and then I can help them to work through it; otherwise it will act as an elastic band to pull that belief into their experience. These beliefs will act as sabotage to you. If you are sceptical about these ideas, check out the increasing amount of scientific evidence that supports the notion of what I'm suggesting here. I can tell you from countless studies that this is true! The following section will help you to work out what they may be and how to work through them.

Analyse your beliefs carefully

Let's get into working out exactly what could potentially hold you back from achieving your objectives. We all have them, little gremlin thoughts that can stop us in our tracks, and unless we deal with them 'up front', they could make our journey much slower and harder to navigate.

What do you think is holding you back?

I would like you to really explore this question. Even if you're feeling pretty clear, I want you to dig deep and come up with anything at all which you think may 'get in the way' or be an excuse for not taking things further. Let's look at some common reasons why people say they can't move forward or are feeling 'trapped'.

On many an occasion, people have said to me, 'My partner isn't supportive, so I'll have to do this on my own and I'm not sure if I can.' In answer to this, I acknowledge that it is much easier to embark upon any venture if you have a supportive environment in which to do it; however, it is not the determining factor. Believe you me, as long as YOU are certain of what you're doing, all else will slot into place. Having been a teacher for many years prior to investing, coaching and mentoring others through this process, I can honestly say that *it isn't ever about anybody else*! If you have ever heard of the phrase 'perception is projection', then you'll know that I'm talking here about your own perceptions being projected out onto someone else. If you can really 'get' this, it will open up your world. For example, if I attended a class in a bad mood and had 'got out of the wrong side of the bed' one day, you could rest assured that my students would reflect this right back at me! I would turn up and there would be a series of pupils being late, forgetting to come to their lesson, lacking practice on their instrument or being just plain grumpy—like me! You can imagine that these were not productive days! On the other hand, when I went out feeling good about myself and with that 'today is going to be a good day' kind of attitude, I would notice how my day would reflect this too. My students would show up on time, have a positive attitude in the lesson, would enjoy their lesson more and end their lesson feeling good about themselves. What I am trying to say is that what you are seeing in your partner is just a reflection of how you feel about yourself. When you say 'my partner isn't supportive', it's because you are not feeling supportive/certain of yourself. I have seen it when I have worked through this particular issue/belief with someone; the transformation has been amazing. I only ever work with the person who has the issue and never the partner because it is not my job to 'fix' the other person. It is more about helping the person who perceives the problem to realise there isn't one, except in their own head!

Family commitments can seem to have a big part to play in determining whether you have the time or energy to go out and do this. If, like many of my clients, you have a young family and want to spend time with them rather than every spare hour on how to acquire, build and run a successful property business, then you need to think carefully about exactly how you're going to do this. Tied in with this are other time constraints, the main one of course being work! If you are employed full-time or work in your own business, a major part of your day will be spent doing this. Work out how much 'spare' time you have and are willing to devote to this new project, then find a strategy which works best for you to fit in with this.

The money factor is one of the biggest restrictions people feel. You are either in the category of people who know they have financial resources...or not! Don't worry, if you feel restricted in this area, it may be that you just can't see a way for yourself right now and need a bit of help to discover options which you may not have known were available to you.

What is your biggest fear around investing in property?
It is very useful to ask yourself this question. I have never met anyone who hasn't been afraid of something! By our very nature, we are motivated either by that which we love or that which we fear. I see my role as helping people to be/get clear and have a healthy motivation towards that which they love rather than be run by fear.

It can sometimes take a while to get to the root fear that you hold around any particular subject; however, it is an incredibly helpful exercise if you can take the time to do it properly. I would suggest you start with a blank piece of paper and write down whatever comes to your mind.

QUESTION: What is my biggest fear
around investing in property?

The next step in this equation is to get down to the one core belief you hold. Can you see a theme running through what you have written down? It may be that you have only written one thing down, or you may have a whole page full of thoughts. To help you with this part, the most common core beliefs people hold around this topic are as follows:

'I'm afraid of losing money.'
'I'm afraid of success.'
'I'm afraid of failure.'
'I'm afraid of losing face.'
'I'm not good enough.'
'I'm not confident.'

What is yours?

One of these will most likely be close to what you have come to your own conclusion about.

The final element to this is to write down a core statement, in the present tense, which describes your feelings in a nutshell. For example:

'I lose money when I invest in property.'
'I lose friends when I am a successful investor.'
'I'm a failure.'
'I'm hopeless at finding deals.'
'I lack confidence in speaking to people.'

When you 'hit' on the right core belief statement for you, I can tell you now it will resonate very strongly with you. You will *know* with absolute certainty that this is the one that will hold you back! If you were to blast this away, then you'd be unstoppable!!

The Belief Box exercise

Now that you have your core 'fear' belief statement, it is time to work on it. First, let me ask you a question: what is a belief? I'll give you my definition. It is something that YOU/I think is true and no longer question. This is great, because if a belief is just something which you've chosen to take on, then you can just as much choose to leave it too! I don't think anybody ever really consciously goes around 'hanging on' to beliefs which don't support them; they are just thoughts that we have picked up on our journey through life and have never given a second thought to.

The trick here, when 'letting go' of such an unsupportive belief, is not just to deny or resist it but to work through and know that it is total rubbish!! You can then replace it with something which *is* supportive and true for you, to enable you to go forward and build your business in a much more positive way. Let me demonstrate what I mean.

I call this exercise The Belief Box exercise. It is a simple yet very powerful little exercise which, when worked on correctly, can help you to change your beliefs and therefore your outlook on the world dramatically. This is a very useful technique when starting out in property or business, or really anything in life if you want to come at it from the best perspective possible.

You will see below a diagram which I have put together to show you how this works. You may find it helpful to do this exercise with a trusted friend or family member, with them asking you the questions and writing down your answers. This gives you the freedom to just think about your answers without having to use another part of your brain to process them and write them down. In it is an example of a belief I worked through with someone. Firstly, you write in your core belief into the 'centre' of the box shape.

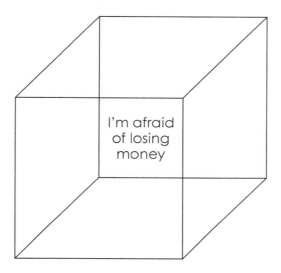

Now, as with any belief we hold, especially a firm belief, there are always other 'supporting beliefs' which make the core belief appear to be real. The edges of the box represent these other beliefs which have helped to do this. You can see below that I have added the other supporting beliefs to each of the sides of the box. You do this by asking yourself the following questions:

Why is the core statement true?
What has happened in my past/childhood in order for me to believe this?
What has happened/is happening in other areas of my life to support this belief?
What have I seen happen to other people which makes this true?

I want you to really dig deep on this. You will probably find several reference points which come up to support your original thought, and they will most likely have occurred throughout your life. In every case I have worked though this exercise with people, it has inevitably led back to something in their early days which has impacted them, and they have then experienced or noticed similar events recurring throughout their life to reinforce this pattern. It is only when you work through it in this way that you become aware of it and how much of a stranglehold it has had over you.

The next part of the exercise is to go through the reasons why each of the statements on the sides of the box is actually complete B***S***!! What?! Yes, you read correctly, why they are BS! This is probably the hardest part of the exercise and yet the most powerful if you can really see through what you have held on to. I have again shown examples below to help you grasp this concept. As you think of reasons to counteract the statements on each side, I'd like you to put a line through each of these statements. Eventually you will have 'knocked away' each side of the box leaving you with the original statement (which no longer has any power).

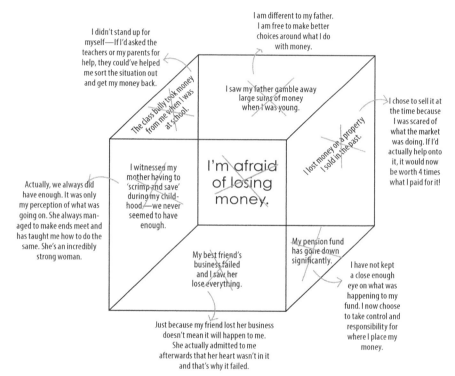

When you do this, you will notice that your attitude starts to shift around the original strongly held belief. You will notice yourself begin to let go of its hold over you. This may happen all of a sudden as you complete this exercise, or more subtly over the course of the next few days or weeks. You will come to feel neutral about this belief, and it will no longer influence you.

The last part of the exercise is to now create a new belief box with a new core belief inside which is totally supportive to you. Ask yourself these following questions:

> What is the opposite of the original belief?
> What would I now like to believe about investing in property/making investment decisions?
> Which belief do I now choose to support me?

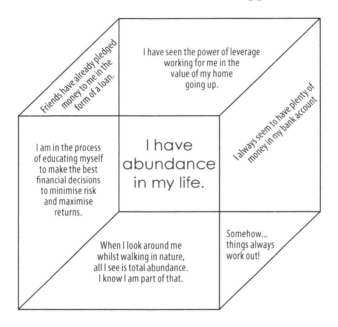

Now add all the reasons why this belief is *already true*! There must be elements in your life where you can already see this being the case; it's just that you never acknowledged them before. After writing these in, you may start to feel a sense of ease and lightness around the subject where there hadn't been before.

The final part of this whole exercise is to ceremoniously destroy the original piece of paper with the unsupportive belief on it, either by burning it outside or tearing it up into pieces and throwing it away, or however you choose. Re-write the new one and put it somewhere prominent so that you can see each it day whilst the new belief sinks in for a while. You will soon start to experience its effects.

If you haven't done so already, I strongly encourage you to do this exercise. It is so simple yet so powerful. Little do we realise how much we are influenced by uncovered and unacknowledged subconscious beliefs.

Procrastination and perfectionism

I see a lot of people who are affected by these fraudulent time-wasters. I too used to feel like I had to have everything just right in order to do anything. What I learnt along the way is that this gets you nowhere very slowly! Of course, there is a major difference between doing things right or wrong, and I am in no way encouraging you to cut corners. It is more about striking a balance between doing enough and then taking action to move you forward in a project.

Waiting for everything to be 'just right'

Being a victim of having to 'line up all the ducks' in order to move along on something can cause great anguish and frustration. You will rarely find a situation which is totally perfect in order to proceed; this is where your 'gut feeling' will come in very useful to help you make a final decision.

Whilst it is true that the market goes in cycles, it is possible to make property investment work whatever the circumstances. For example, I made one of the best purchases right at the 'top' of the market before the credit crunch hit. I had negotiated a deal on a 6 bedroom HMO in Sheffield, one of the UK's largest university towns. We were buying it for £260K, and its true value was £325K. The property needed refurbishment and the proper alterations to make it compliant as a student HMO property. We bought the property and spent about £20K to do the corrective works and then refinanced (at 80% LTV – Loan To Value) the property to the £325K value, leaving in only the £20k refurbishment costs and buying costs. This property produced a cash flow of £600 pcm at the time and has fared even better since we bought it due to the market conditions over the last few years and interest rates going so low. This demonstrates that you will never know exactly when the right time to invest will be or when the market is 'just right'; you only have to know what you're doing when you do it!

Analysis paralysis

I often find that when someone has been looking at all the different options in terms of investing, they can become almost obsessed with trying to 'get it right' and make sure everything is perfect before stepping out. This literally stops people in their tracks and can act as the biggest brake. The effect is that they don't seem to be able to 'see the wood for the trees' anymore and have lost sight of their original goal. They spend so much time analysing deals and checking out which is the best route to go down that they never actually begin.

I refer to this as 'rabbit caught in headlights' mode! When you no longer feel confident in what you're doing due to having been bombarded with information, the end result can be that you don't do anything at all! This often comes when there is a lack of alignment between what you are thinking and how you feel. You are too 'stuck in your head' and not listening to what your heart and gut are feeling.

This confirms that too much research can send you a little potty! Of course, I reiterate the point that you must do research and due diligence, just avoid getting stuck there by having a plan and really knowing where you're heading.

You don't have to get it right; you just have to get it going!

Thinking back to when we first started investing, we had a rough idea of what we wanted to achieve and had devised a very 'head in the clouds' kind of plan to make it happen; however, much of what we did in the early days was in the 'aim, fire, ready!' approach rather than being totally organised about things. We were almost complete novices when we first started investing— only having bought two of our own homes (one at a time!) before but never looking at property from an investment point of view. We just knew that, for us, property was a good idea and decided to go for it with the little advice we had been given. Even knowing what I know now, I am very glad we took the leap of faith. If we had tried to make sure everything was 'perfect' to start with, then we would almost certainly never have got involved.

I do now totally subscribe to the idea that getting the right help and having a well thought out plan when investing in property is worth its weight in gold, hence why I started my own business, Why Property Works™. The reason for starting this business was that I would love to have had someone to help us navigate the way properly when we first started off who could have seen things objectively and viewed the process through experienced eyes. I am certain that our portfolio would have built up in a very different way with this knowledge, and that is what I am now able to do with my clients.

Give up flogging a dead horse!

There are occasions when I meet people who have been to all the courses, read all the books, are in financial difficulty or other tricky life situations and are looking to property investment as 'the answer'. With the best will in the world, if you come to this business starting off on the 'wrong foot', nothing you do will make it happen. I have already been through working out the practicalities and certain aspects of mindset which can 'get in the way', but sometimes you have to acknowledge that it just may not be the right time for you.

If all the indicators show it is not for you right now, then STOP!

If you don't listen to your gut feeling (which may be telling you to stop), you may end up causing yourself more stress and aggravation than originally anticipated. When I worked with the people I mentioned earlier who came to property out of desperation that they could resolve their financial issues from it, the problem was more often than not that there was a lot of fear attached to their decision to invest. They were not coming from a place of clarity and certainty that this was absolutely the right course of action for them to take. They had heard that other people became wealthy through property; therefore, it would be the same for them. The sad fact was that in these cases, this was just not true at that time. It felt like they were trying to fit a square peg into a round hole, and it just did not fit. I now make sure there is true alignment before I work with a client to ensure a 'best fit' scenario. I will only work with people I know I can help.

I felt that these people were living in a world of disillusionment. They had heard stories of what is possible and what others had achieved without having explored what the options really were for them. We all come from different backgrounds, walks of life and levels of experience, and we are not all destined to follow the same path; therefore, I feel it is crucial to know whether property is right for you from the start so that you can concentrate on what is truly best for you.

You'll be doing yourself a favour, really!

If you can work out and focus on that which you really enjoy and are passionate about and this works out not to be property, then you are far better off concentrating on that. It will feel like the right decision, and you will be much happier for it. You will most likely discover that the more you do what you love to do—rather than what you have to do in order to make money—the money will come anyway! This in turn will mean that you have more resources to put into property investment when the time is right.

By doing this, you will actually save your energy and nerves and enable yourself to come from a much better place when you do start to consider property again.

It may only mean 'not for now'

If circumstances dictate that property may not be the best route for you to go down right now, this does not mean that you will not ever be able to. The mere fact that you have an interest in property is a good first step; it's just that there must be alignment in other areas of your life in order for it to happen for you as you wish it to.

You may find yourself a few years down the line in very different circumstances which mean that you can now easily consider property investment as an option, so don't ever 'give up' on it completely. My intention behind this section is so that you avoid the trap of feeling like you are flogging a dead horse in your pursuits.

6.

LET'S CUT THE CR*P

→ The myths around
the property industry ←

Let's 'Cut the C**p!'

The myths around the property investment industry

AS A PRE-CURSOR TO THE rest of this chapter, I felt compelled to 'get real' about certain aspects of the world of property investment, and the following is my take on things. I feel that there is an awful lot of 'smoke and mirrors' out there, and I wish to clear the view so that you may navigate your way safely through what some may call 'shark infested waters'! Ultimately, property investing is an unregulated industry, and you need to be certain of what you are getting yourself into well before you get into it! If this chapter can serve as an aide to sort out the wheat from the chaff for you, then my intention has been fulfilled.

Everyone and anyone can do it

When you first come across property investment as a good idea, there will be many people both online and offline who tell you that it's a great idea and to get involved. Of course, I'd be a hypocrite if I didn't agree! What I do object to, however, is the way that people are told and what they are told. With a profusion of property-related exhibitions, courses, seminars, blogs, books, forums online, networking events, etc., property investment can be made to sound easy; some claim that you can start off with potentially little or no money, no experience or only a little of your time. Except for a small minority of people, this is just blatantly not true. I have said before that it takes a certain mindset and a special skill set to be able to just start out in property from nothing and no experience and make it work. The number of people whose heads are just not in the right 'space' at the outset far outweighs those who are.

It takes a very particular set of circumstances, both financial and personal in order to just go out there and make it happen. Property investment is sold to the public as 'the dream' that many of them will aspire to. They are told it provides income, long-term wealth, a secure future and status, all of which is true. However, the problem does not lie in this type of information being told to the public; it lies in the way people are being 'sold' that dream when it may not be appropriate for them at that particular time. Amidst the 'hype' and promotion, it is important to keep your feet firmly on the ground and ensure alignment before taking any course of action.

I agree with the statement that anyone can do it—just not that everyone should do it, as I've said earlier.

You can do it in your 'spare' time
Unless you have subscribed to being on the whole an 'armchair' investor or someone who has a sourcing agent to work for you on finding and managing deals, property is not strictly a 'spare time' occupation. I speak here for myself and the countless people I have met whose original intention it was to just do property 'on

the side' and then discovered that it takes a whole lot more time and effort than they had originally anticipated.

This is especially true in the early stages of your investing career where you are literally learning the ropes—it can be all-consuming. As already covered, you can't expect to become an expert investor overnight. It takes practice, patience, learning from the school of hard knocks and sheer determination. You cannot replace the 'hard work' element unless you are getting someone else to do this for you. Even then, this is a risky strategy unless *you* really know that they know what they're doing! This only comes from experience and so almost produces a 'chicken and egg' situation. I have worked with novice investors who have thought they were saving the 'time' element by outsourcing the deal-finding and refurbishing element, only to be seriously stung by those they had trusted, purely because those 'professionals' hadn't really known what they claimed to know.

Financial freedom is just around the corner

This is a common claim from 'experts' who would sell you the dream of property investment. It is again a far cry from the truth of the matter for the vast majority. The number of those who start out in property investment with a view to becoming 'financially free' and who actually achieve it at all is tiny and even smaller within a short space of time. A few more go on to become financially independent within 5–10 years, and the largest proportion of people who started out initially on this track fall by the wayside, either turning to other methods of creating wealth or stopping altogether. This leads to feelings of massive disappointment and frustration for a lot of people. Let's face it, only a very small percentage of people *ever* become financially independent through any means, let alone in 2–5 years! How, then, can this be pitched to so many knowing full well that so few will ever actually achieve it?

The absolute exception to the rule is this: when all the factors that I have described above are in place and acted upon, then a determined individual will pull it off. My advice is that if the person/company promoting such a claim of success cannot prove it substantially through a number of genuine testimonials of what people have actually achieved, evidential proof and percentage success rates, then question carefully!

My approach is much more slow-burn and slow-build (the tortoise versus the hare approach, 'slow and steady wins the race', remember!), which leads to sustainability over the long-term. If you are methodical in your approach, have a good plan and achieve steady and progressive growth, then this will serve you much better in the long run. Why rush into something when you are likely to crash and burn when you could do so much better taking your time, analysing where you're at and where you'd like to get to and making proper headway in a direction that is right for you over a timescale that is realistic and you know is achievable.

The truth about the property investment industry

Here is what to watch out for and be wary of when you are thinking of getting involved in property or are looking to work with a particular person or company.

Much of it will be 'hype'

If you have looked into or are already involved in property, you may or may not know that a lot of what you read and come across is pure and simple hype. Whichever angle you look from, whether it is a property course, a stand at an exhibition, estate agent, deal sourcer or even a fellow investor, a huge amount of what you hear will be somebody trying to 'tell you what you want to hear'. Whether that is the impressive lifestyle, property portfolio, best deal or whatever, a lot of what you will come across will be 'noise'.

If you ever attend any of the big property exhibitions, you will come across a myriad of stands that will try to entice you in. Of course, this type of situation is good for you to explore the options open to you but is all too easy to become distracted in. The promotion of investing in foreign property has shot through the roof in the last decade or so, and these particular forms of investment need to be scrutinised with a very fine tooth comb. I have known many an investor fall foul of this type of promotion, mainly because they do not understand what they are being offered, they have no idea about the laws or regulations in another country and they literally give their power away to a relatively unknown source in the promise and hope that they know what they're doing. It is my belief that it is surely best to understand what property investment is all about in your own country first (which is challenging enough), let alone be seduced into a romantic notion of cocktails at sunset in some exotic location in the hope that it is a 'hotspot' and will make you a fortune. Undoubtedly there will be some good prospects abroad, though it takes real experience to be able to sift them out.

I know that there are a lot of people who have become disillusioned and frustrated with the number of companies or individuals who offer services which just didn't match up to their initial expectations. The tactics of baffling you with information can make you feel inferior and prevent you from asking the right questions because you think they must 'know it all'. You may feel bombarded with information and have no clue where to turn for sound advice on how to do things properly. Beware the bold promises and claims and always check them out. If what you are hearing sounds too good to be true, then it most likely is. I believe it is time for a 'wake up, shake up' in this industry. The fact is that the people who are operating in this way are not necessarily conscious about making sure that what they have to offer actually aligns with the consumer. Their message is so powerful that it entices some members of their audience in the wrong way. It's time for a change! Ultimately, however, we must remember that the obligation does not lie with these companies to necessarily change their way of doing things; it is up to us to take responsibility for our own actions. A good analogy to describe what I am talking about is the phrase 'prognosis without diagnosis is malpractice'. This essentially sums up what I mean by the alignment process I refer to in this context. You wouldn't expect a doctor to prescribe a course of medication if they hadn't first determined your condition, would you?!

Look for 'grounded' enthusiasm based on facts. People and organisations who are operating ethically and who concentrate on their clients' satisfaction and needs will shine through. They will often be very modest about what they can do for their clients/customers and don't need to shout it from the rooftops. There's a great saying that goes 'what you do speaks so loudly I cannot hear what you say'. This is a good one to remember as the people who are genuinely concerned and have the best intentions are mainly 'getting on with it'.

Watch out for who is getting the best deal
There are property investment companies, sourcing agents, BMV (Below Market Value) companies, estate agents, etc., who all will tell you that they have the best deals or 'just the deal for you'. When presented with any 'deal', you absolutely *must* run

your own research and due diligence on it, regardless of where it has come from—even if you know that source to be reliable. A number of those mentioned above take the best deals for themselves or a very select few clients, offering the 'crumbs' to the rest of their database or other client banks. A glossy brochure or email suggesting fantastic returns and/or little or no money needed must be investigated, quite literally, for all it's worth! I am pleased to say that I have prevented many a client from investing in something they knew nothing or little about, which on the surface sounded great but when, after further inspection, was not all it was cracked up to be. It really is a 'buyer beware' marketplace, and you need to know what you're getting yourself into.

Regardless of its source, you must be really certain of what you're being sold. Ask yourself, 'Does it really stack up?' If you can't answer 'yes' to that, don't buy!

Contrary to popular belief, the majority of property investment companies, estate agents and letting agents DO NOT know what constitutes a 'good deal'. Please, please, PLEASE do not be fooled by those who seem to know better than you about what is a good deal or the right deal for you. Even those who are fellow investors may have a very different way of doing things than you or are just plain wrong in the way they go about it. Never be fooled by hearing the words 'this is a good deal' without going over it with a fine-tooth comb yourself—more help on this later!

Again, in the early days, we fell prey to a couple of people who we believed knew better than us when we first started out. We were admittedly very green around the edges, and when you let yourself be lured into a false sense of security by people whom you trust to know better than you, this can be a very dangerous place to be. We landed up investing in a couple of deals (one of which I described earlier) that ended up losing us a significant amount of money and causing a great deal of head and heartaches and stress along the way. It was down to the fact that they did not in fact know better than us and were only interested in making a lot of money on the sale of each one under the guise of each one being 'discounted' heavily. We were looking for an 'easy' way to be involved in property and have the 'hard work' done for us. We take full responsibility for the fact that we should have indeed known better and that we were at total liberty to walk away. However, as it stands, it was probably the biggest and best 'learning experience' we could ever have had in how NOT to do things, and we have since gone on to make far better decisions and build our portfolio on substantiated evidence and thorough due diligence.

Beware the 'sharks'
These are people who are mainly in business to make money out of the unwary and ill-informed. As per the story above, it is easy to be lulled into a false sense of security when you do not know what you are doing, and this is the easiest way to be 'bitten'. If I am really honest, it was down to the fact that we were being somewhat slack and a little greedy in thinking we could make property work just by trusting other people and not doing enough of the 'leg work' ourselves. This is where the 'sharks' take advantage of others' naivety, greed and laziness and sell their property services or products to the unsuspecting public. There are a number of examples of companies who have taken advantage in this way, which you can find for yourself on the internet, some of whom are now (thankfully) out of business. These are classic cases in point where literally hundreds, if not thousands, of people were taken in on an unsustainable strategy, relying solely on growth in the marketplace without protection for the downside, thus leading to lost capital, negative cash flow and personal bankruptcies, not to mention a

whole heap of heartache. This must teach us to do better than to blindly trust the 'sharp suits' and 'smooth talking' and to dig much deeper before committing to anything.

I always recommend checking individuals and companies out thoroughly. Even just 'Googling' someone can uncover a multitude of things. Make sure you look beyond the first few pages as well as references in other countries if applicable. Websites such as www.companycheck.co.uk and www.company-director-check.co.uk are also worth researching Limited (LTD) Companies (in the UK) and their Directors. It is interesting what can show up. There are lots of other ways to investigate who you are dealing with; it just takes a little nous and imagination. To ascertain an individual's net worth is much harder, if not impossible, really. You can only go on the information you are given and as much of what you have researched yourself. You can never really know somebody's bank balance, property or share portfolio or other assets because, quite frankly, it is no one else's business. This is where the intangible element of trust must ultimately come in. The motto is basically 'check out everybody you intend to do business with, large or small'. At the end of the day, once you have a picture of where someone is at as much as you possibly can, it then boils down to sheer gut instinct as to whom to trust. Be guided by this every time!

The Pareto Principle (AKA the 80/20 rule) – the real story

You've heard the statistics. Out of every 100 people who attend an event, be that a seminar, weekend exhibition, webinar, etc., 80% will walk away and do nothing, while 20% will begin on a certain path. Out of the remaining 20, 80% (16 people) will again not actually achieve very much, and the last 20% (4 people) will go on to do something. Yes, you've guessed right, out of those final 4 people, 80% will do quite well, and only 20% (<1 person!) will make it to the ultimate goal they set out to achieve. This is really quite shocking. When you take into account that information and education in this arena can be highly priced, it seems such a shame when only a very small minority succeed. This, I believe, is true across all 'wealth-creation' industries and goes to show why the people or companies who are set up to sell this type of training do very well out of it, and yet a large proportion of people they work with do not succeed as they would like. There is an alarming imbalance between the two sides—living proof that the need for alignment between client circumstances and services offered needs to be in play.

When they talk about their 'success rates', make sure you ask for proof, actual evidence and real testimonials that can back up the statistics they are claiming. Also, check whether any of their clients are willing to talk to you about their experiences. More often than not, wealth-creation sellers won't actually tell you their true levels of success as that would probably put you off buying!! Again, it can be very hard to determine this fully, but any organisation worth their salt should know their true success rate and really be screening those they work with to ensure there is a 'correct fit' between what they do/have to offer and what the person wants.

My mission in my business is to reverse the 80/20 rule and for there to be an absolute minimum of 80% of my clients to be achieving what they set out to achieve by working with me. By helping people to discover their true purpose and values and align this with their method of wealth-creation, I have found that this holistic approach ensures a best-fit scenario and has resulted in the successful reversal of this statistic with well over 80% of my clients actually achieving the results they seek. I will only work with those I know I can help to the best of my knowledge.

The 'gurus' do NOT know what's best for YOU

I use the term 'guru' to mean people who have a certain level of property or other wealth-building experience and now train and guide others to follow in their footsteps, to aim to achieve similar results as they have. It seems we have developed almost a 'guru' culture, where people flock to various courses and seminars accepting other people's ideologies and strategies almost without question. This leads us to ignore our own true purpose, values and needs around the creation of wealth. With fewer than 5% of people achieving what they set out to with these methods, it creates a syndrome that could be described as 'trying to fit a square peg into a round hole'. This leads to feelings of misalignment, procrastination and, in the worst cases, ill-informed decision-making, which can result in financial losses, thus compromising family and work life and putting financial futures at risk. Whilst I am sure that these people have a great deal of experience, the point is not all about *what* they know and can pass on, rather whether their knowledge and methods are *right* for other people.

All that glitters...

For sure, there are people and companies in this industry who do operate in a sound, ethical way and know that their product or service is relevant for those who come into their organisation. There are some, however, which you need to be wary of. Watch out for bold, unsubstantiated claims and promises, which are not necessarily backed up, either in terms of the number of properties someone owns or has had dealings with, as well as the number of satisfied clients who have worked with them. People who look like they've 'made it' can be very persuasive, and it is easy to be 'wowed' by the image you see before you. It is also good to note that due to changes in the law, financial industry, market conditions, etc., a strategy which worked well for someone ten years ago may not work now, even though they still endorse it. Those people I have met and worked with who have been truly successful haven't necessarily needed to brag about it. They seem to automatically exude an air of confidence whilst remaining modest. These are the people you really want to learn from. Trust your gut feeling and remember to do as much research and due diligence on someone as you possibly can before going ahead and working with them. If a deal sounds fantastic, please, please, please make sure you research it thoroughly—the title of this section says it all. I have worked with too many people who have been 'sucked in' by amazing-sounding ideas and deals only to be truly burnt. After all, would you commit potentially hundreds of thousands of pounds on the recommendation of someone you knew nothing about? That would be like agreeing to take flight with someone you didn't even know was a qualified pilot!

Ensure that the person or business is operating legally. Check out whether the address they provide you with checks out as a properly registered address and whether you have access to help when you need it. If you find it very hard to get hold of them, why is this?

Check out, as far as you can, their background. How long have they been in operation? Is there evidence of this? What other sorts of businesses have they been involved with in the past—did they have a good reputation? Have they been involved in anything fraudulent? Be fairly wary of any business which has been operating for less than a year; check them out thoroughly and ask them to provide back-up evidence of any claims they make. Businesses that are 'new' could be perfectly legitimate; however, they could also be a cover-up for another business having gone under previously. Bear in mind that Companies House will have limited information on brand new companies.

One caveat here is not to mistake the fact that people who have gone bankrupt in the past (as long as they are open about it) are in some way not worth listening to or even working with. If they now stand in front of you as someone who has made it out of that situation and learned a heap along the way, then they may very well be just the person who can help you. As long as they are not covering up the fact and pretending to be something they are not, this is fine.

Where they make a lot of their money

If you look closely at most of the 'big' names in property and think for a minute where a lot of their money comes from, you will see clearly that selling deals and/or information or education brings in a great deal of revenue. There is of course nothing wrong with this if the consumer is getting what they expect and want from the transaction. If you examine closely the intention behind the delivery of the information, this will give you the best clue. If it is to genuinely inform and give people the best 'knowledge' from their perspective and act as a magnet to attract the right people to work with and they then make sure there is an alignment process rather than just a sales pitch, that's fine. If their intention is solely to gain proceeds towards their business and/or other operations at the expense of the consumer, that is when the transaction is flawed.

There is no doubt that the fees charged for different events by different people vary massively, and the value gained is down to individual experience. It is always interesting to note again the number of success stories vs. the number of people who attend these events. This boils down again to the 80/20 rule and goes to demonstrate the almost 'herd' mentality which drives people to them looking for the 'answer'. The sad fact is that for a large number of people, it just isn't. They are deluding themselves if they think that a person/people on a stage telling them what to do and how to do it is right for them—they must search for the answer first in themselves. The problem is that there are very few mechanisms and little or no screening in place to help people recognise exactly what is right for them, thus saving them from shelling out lots of money and time on deals, courses or any other information which may not be worth their while.

Does it 'fit' with you?

Just because they've 'done it', it doesn't mean that you have to, should, or even can! I mean this with the greatest of respect for all the reasons already mentioned in this book. I once heard Richard Farleigh (a previous 'Dragon' from the *Dragon's Den* series on BBC2) speak at a business event and say that if you took ten people and gave them exactly the same set of resources and circumstances to start up something new, only one would end up making it. I was so relieved to hear that someone else shared my sentiments. Is it any wonder then that the success rate is so low in this industry given the fact that there are so many different factors to take into consideration? The most critical factor to watch out for in yourself is the 'needy' feeling and thinking that something is the 'answer to all your prayers' just because it can fulfil this need. If you are really honest with yourself, you will stop for a minute to ask yourself whether this really is the best course of action for you to take or whether it is best to wait and maybe consider other options.

If you decide to go ahead with a particular course of action, make sure that you feel completely aligned with what is being offered/taught and that this is a 'best fit' for your investment objectives. Remember to look and ask for evidence-backed claims and proof of statistics in the form of 'kosher' testimonials. Any well-meaning person or company will be able to deliver this.

Be true to yourself

Stick to your main objective, remember your 'why' and keep your head down!

This really is a golden rule which you must follow. It is all too easy to be distracted and go off course either when you first start out or even along the way as a more experienced investor. I call this the 'shiny object' syndrome. Trying to follow too many different avenues of wealth creation or property strategies can lead to a serious delay in getting what you set out to achieve. The key is to focus and stick to the path of action which works for you. My most successful clients have been those who have become very clear on exactly what it is they want to achieve, have a big reason for doing it and just get on with it! This really is common sense and will stand you in good stead. I can re-member one client who came to me with an existing portfolio of 15 properties which were almost cash flow neutral and who wanted to change strategy to bring in more cash flow. He decided upon a strategy and focussed on this during his time with me. He ended up growing his portfolio with a different strategy than he had before by turning large 'freehold' blocks of flats into in-dividual 'leasehold' units, which individually generated decent monthly returns. He was able to recycle his funds efficiently and could bring his son into the business to help him grow it further. This just goes to show that focus is crucial to ending up where you'd like to be!

At the other end of the spectrum, I met another person whilst taking my son swimming. We got chatting and he asked what I did. It turned out that he was looking for just one property to become part of his business but also knew it would be wise to come from a long-term investment perspective too. Having no experience in this field, he called on me to help him find the best type of property in the area he was concentrating in. He had originally been looking for 2 bedroom flats for around £120-130K with a rental of £550 pcm. Now it doesn't take much to work out that this was not going to produce the best return. After working together a few times, we identified an ideal property in a fabulous location which was absolutely fit for purpose. The flat had been on the market for a little while and had dropped from £110,000 to £99,950. It was fully refurbished and in a decent, well-kept block. He was looking to purchase within a short time-frame and so I suggested going in at £81,250. He was flabbergasted and didn't think it would go anywhere near that figure. After a small amount of negotiation, it came in at £84,250. It just goes to show that even when you're looking for one deal, it pays to know what you're doing!

As soon as you dip into the world of property investing, you will come across myriads of different strategies and people with opinions as to which option you should take. Remember always that just because someone else is doing it does not mean it is necessarily right for you. Once you know what you'd like to achieve, stick to your guns and seek help and advice from those you know and can trust to enable you to achieve it. If you are consistent in this approach, you *will* get there!

Sift/filter through all the 'advice' and information
Literally, when you 'cut the c**p', your best course of action will be revealed to you. You will root out what works and is best for you. Make sure you are honest with yourself about what 'sits right' and go with that feeling every time. If your head spins, listen to your gut feeling rather than getting wrapped up in your

thoughts. I cannot stress enough how important this point is for making decisions.

Only YOU know what's best for YOU

When all is said and done, the person you can trust the most is, of course, YOU! Nobody holds your interests closer to your heart than you, so why would you entrust some of your biggest life decisions to anyone else? Of course, once you have made the decision, then it is a good idea to enlist someone with whom you feel aligned to help you execute that objective. However, beware that it is all too simple to give your power away to someone else in the first place if you are not careful.

Learn to listen to your own intuition (yes, even you who is thinking you don't have this 'sixth sense'!) and it will stand you in very good stead. Once you have mastered this art, you must then trust your own judgement. One client who came to me swore blind that he was purely an 'analytical creature' and didn't know what 'intuition' felt like. We discussed the subject at length, and then I thought there's no substitute for actually experiencing this phenomenon and so we began to 'walk the talk' and actually helped him to become aware of this in himself. I was delighted when, several months later, he rang me and announced that he'd 'got it'! He was talking in terms of things 'feeling right' and 'just knowing' that it was a good deal. I was over the moon as you can imagine.

So, learn to sniff out the BS, trust your instincts and you'll be a long way towards becoming a successful investor!

7. Property Investment as a Business

Property investment as a business

Treat each property as a mini-business – it is

YOU MAY OR MAY NOT be aware that a number of people don't treat the thought of property investing as a business. Even some of those I have worked with and come across over the years who already own property do not necessarily know how to run a portfolio thinking of it as a business. If you think about it, when you are investing precious resources, such as your time, money, other people's money, etc., why wouldn't you think of it like a business?

A reason for every property

When setting up and running your portfolio, you absolutely must know the reason for each property being in it. What I mean by this is rather than buying a property just because it looks nice, is in a convenient location for you or will be a good topic of conversation at a dinner party, the real underlying reason for its purchase must be at the forefront of your mind. If you require cash flow, then your predominant thoughts will be on where and how to obtain the best cash flowing properties. If you want to flip (i.e., buy, do up and sell on for profit), then find a location which will allow you to do this, whichever market you are buying in. If your objective is to build up a pension pot of £3,000 pcm in order for you to retire comfortably at age 55, then there must be a very specific purchase plan to enable you to do this allowing also for the rising cost of living—exactly as you would have with a pension.

If you do not have a clear reason for buying any one property, then you shouldn't be buying it! If you were to buy a property for £125,000 which achieves a rent of £600 pcm and after all costs you are left with £50 positive cash flow at the end of each month, you may not think this is too bad. If, however, your objective is to create a minimum of 8% cash-on-cash return p.a., then you have failed miserably as £50 pcm will only yield you 1.7% p.a.! We'll go into working out the numbers in a minute. This is based on you buying it for full market value and having put in £35,000 in total of your own money. You would have had to negotiate a significant discount or be buying in a completely different area in order to achieve such a return. This is the importance of knowing why you want to buy.

Think of the bigger picture view and work backwards from there in terms of what you'll need to do and buy in order to achieve that goal.

Due diligence and research

As this is not a complete 'how to' book on the exact methodology of all the details around buying property, this section is more of a reminder that this is a crucial element of any purchase you make (i.e., business decision!). The basic requirements of due diligence and research are to know your strategy and have a defined plan to work to, work out which area is best suited for these needs, research that area thoroughly and determine which properties will fit the bill within the area you have chosen. Also, you must know how to analyse which properties you want to go and see, what to look for when you're there, how to figure out costs and therefore what offer you should make. At the same time, you should be finding out about which team of people you're going to use for the purchase process, how you're going to manage the refurbishment (if needed) and management of the property, etc., etc.—the list goes on! As you can see, there is far more to it than I can cover here. I merely want to make the point that it is one of the most important aspects to investing in property. Get this wrong at your peril! There is so much I could write; I feel there is a whole other book in me!

Overestimate costs and underestimate values

It is good practice, however experienced you are, to have a healthy attitude towards how much things could cost on your projects. As we all know, costs are prone to spiral on property if you're not careful, and you'd be wise to err on the side of caution every time.

When you first visit a property, make a note of everything that needs doing so that when you come to work out the numbers, you have a good rough idea of what costs may be involved. If you are completely new to it all, ask the experts. Don't be afraid to get on the phone to builders, plumbers, roofers, etc. to give you a rough estimate to begin with based on the area you are working in. Bear in mind that a builder's day rate in Manchester, for example, will be significantly different to one in London—as will the price of materials in some cases.

Know what your costs are at each stage of the project so you can keep control of them, otherwise you run the risk of going way over budget and blowing the deal out of the water. When you have a clear understanding of costs, overestimate them and then set them against underestimated values of what you think you may achieve on a re-sale or re-finance model. If you don't do this, you may end up being bitterly disappointed. I worked with a client who had allocated £70,000 of their own money into a particular deal only to go over by £31,000!! Ouch! This was an incredibly harsh 'learning' as the property then didn't achieve what they had originally anticipated for it. The moral of this story is this: if it works when you have calculated the figures in the way I have described, if you then subsequently achieve better results than you expected, i.e., lower costs and better end values, then you can really celebrate.

You make your money at the beginning, not at the end!
It is a complete myth to think that you make money on property either when you come to sell or refinance it. The true money is made at the outset. This means buying the property at the right price! This simple truth is astoundingly overlooked by a lot of investors who seem to think it's all about property going up in value over the longer term. Whilst we would always like to think the market will go up, events in the past and also very recent history have taught us that this most certainly is not always the case, and we absolutely need to protect ourselves from the word go.

Let's say that a property is on the market for £100,000 and needs work. Once completed, that property will be worth £125,000. The cost of the work is likely to be £20,000. If you were to pay the asking price, you will eventually be 'in' for the full amount of what it's worth—a pretty dangerous place to be if the market drops. If, however, you were to buy that property for 70% of its current market value (i.e., £70,000, which is 56% of its end value of £125,000), then you will be in for a total of approximately £95,000 with all costs in. This is infinitely more attractive and robust against any fall in the market and enables you to add value to your purchase. The general philosophy is to buy for a 'wholesale' price, improve the property in order to add value to it and then sell or refinance the property for a 'retail' price. It's simple business sense, isn't it?!

Know your numbers!

It never ceases to amaze me when I begin to work with people that plenty do not properly understand the financial aspects of investing in property. With such an important decision to make regarding so much money, why oh why do people leave this section so low down the list of priorities to comprehend? I would imagine that because we are not normally taught these types of processes at school or by our parents, the idea of what makes a good investment is not within our mindset. It is, therefore, absolutely vital that you learn and refine this part until you know it inside out. The following explanations are a good basic start to what you will need to know. Please note that there are more advanced calculations which would be beneficial to you, however the nature of this book is meant to give you an overview, not an in-depth maths lesson!

ROI (Return On Investment) and ROTI (Return On Time Invested)

An ROI is the amount you will be making on any money you invest in a deal. It is exactly like the interest you receive on any money deposited in a bank account. This is a basic calculation and makes for a good starting point. If you were to buy a property for £100,000 and received £6,000 p.a. gross rent, then you would be receiving a return of 6% (£6,000 / £100,000 = 0.06. then 0.06 x 100 = 6%). If you put £100,000 in a bank account receiving 4% gross interest, then you would receive £4,000 p.a.—simple. One factor that many people miss out of the equation is the return on the time they invest into completing a deal. This is known as ROTI. If you have spent 30 hours of your own time into putting a deal together and you value your time, then you must factor an 'hourly rate' into the equation. Let's say this time is worth £20 p.h. then you have put an extra £600 on the bottom line of your figures. If you value it at £50 p.h., then it equates to £1,500—a significant difference. This will help you make the decision about whom you employ for which part of the whole process and where your time is best spent. Another way of looking at it would be that ROTI can also relate to the amount of time you've invested versus the amount you make in profit. For example, if you make £20K total profit and have spent a total of 40 hours putting the deal together and finalising it, you have made £500 p.h.

Yield vs. TRR (True Rate of Return)

Yield is the calculation of the total gross rental income p.a. divided by the property value. We have touched on it just above, but another example would be if you received a monthly rent of £750, this would equate to £9,000 p.a., and if the property was worth £140,000, then the yield figure would be £9,000 / £140,000 = 0.064 then 0.064 x 100 = 6.4% return. This figure on its own may look quite good; however, when we compare it to the TRR, we get a completely different picture. A TRR is where you calculate the numbers based on the true costs of the property set-up against the true income you will receive. It is slightly more complicated in its structure but gives you a much truer picture of that particular property deal. Let's take the same property and work out the TRR figures. I'll keep the numbers very straightforward just to illustrate the point.

Purchase Price	£140,000	
Deposit (@ 25%)	£35,000	+
Costs to purchase (incl. valuation, stamp duty, legals, broker, etc.)	£5,000	=
Therefore total money in	£40,000	
Annual rent	£9,000	−
Annual mortgage interest (based on 75% LTV int. only at 6% int. rate)	£6,300	−
Annual management fee (based on 10% of gross rent)	£900	−
Annual operating costs & expenses (based on 10% of gross rent)	£900	=
Therefore total annual cash flow	£900	

If we now do the same calculation based on the annual cash flow divided by the total money into the deal we have a very different story. £900 / £40,000 = 0.023 then 0.023 x 100 = 2.3% return. Hmmm, all of a sudden this doesn't look as good any more, does it?! A 2.3% return is about the same as you'd achieve in a decent savings account currently, and that's an awful lot easier! Of course, the argument is that a property can increase significantly in value over time, therefore producing a very decent return on capital. However, when viewing from a purely business perspective, you have to ensure the return is there from the outset, otherwise you fall into the trap of *relying* on the market rising rather than making the deal work for you regardless of the market. Many 'traditional' investment decisions have been made purely on yield calculations. I always advocate also working out the TRR as this will give you a much truer picture of the investment you are making. Hopefully you can now see that this is a much more business-like way of approaching a potential deal. It gives you scope to anticipate fluctuations in rent, interest rate, operating costs, etc., and how this will affect the overall end result.

Without meaning to offend any estate or letting agents reading this, many will make recommendations on certain properties based solely on the yield. The reason this is such an unreliable way of making a decision is that it doesn't address these multiple other factors you need to account for. Make sure you work out your calculations correctly and always based on the TRR. My golden 'rule of thumb' is this: if I'm not making at least 8% minimum TRR on a deal, then I don't do it (normally significantly more these days—though this would be a good starting point for you). Why would you go to all the hassle, expense and time to make barely above what the banks will give you anyway? You want to at least have a decent recompense for your efforts and a buffer to safeguard your investment.

'Wash Its Face' calculations

This term is commonly used in the industry to mean whether a property will 'look after itself' in terms of the amount of rent coming in versus the amount of expenses going out. Ideally you don't just want it to 'look after itself', you want a decent return too (unless you are investing purely for capital growth); however, this is purely an exercise on the principle. This is a very basic formula designed to help you work out whether a property is even worth the time of day to go see.

Let's take the same property again worth £140,000. Begin with the property value and then work out the amount of mortgage you can obtain in total (the level of LTV). Multiply this number by the interest rate you'll be paying and divide it by 12 to give you a monthly figure. This is then multiplied by the rate of rental coverage the lender will want to see. What does this look like?

Property value	£140,000	×
0.75 (mortgage amount of 75% LTV)	£105,000	×
0.06 (interest rate at 6% interest only)	£6,300	/
12 (to give a monthly mortgage figure)	£525	×
1.25 (125% rental coverage needed by the lender)	£656	

This figure of £656 tells you that the rent of £750 is enough to cover the requirements of the lender and is a good place to start when considering a property.

Another calculation is the 'Reverse Wash Its Face'. Conversely, this exercise can be used to determine the maximum property value you can look up to when considering the amount of rent you'll achieve. Let's take the £750 rent example and analyse. Firstly, you take the monthly rental figure and divide it by the lender's rental coverage rate. Next, you multiply that figure by 12 to gain an annual mortgage interest figure. Then you divide this number by the interest rate and finally divide it again by the loan to value of the mortgage you are able to get. Here is a worked example.

Monthly rent	£750	/
1.25 (125% rental coverage amount)	£600	×
12 (to give an annual mortgage figure)	£7,200	/
0.06 (interest rate at 6% int. only to give you a maximum mortgage amount)	£120,000	/
0.75 (75% LTV in this case) against a value of	£160,000	

‑ou will see here that based on the rental income of £750 pcm, you are actually allowed to borrow £120,000 based on a property worth £160,000.

This always astounds me as, based on a traditional method of buying property, the rate of return on this property would then be so low (and may even cost you money each month!) it wouldn't even be worth bothering to look at! If, however, you know what you are doing, you could still make this a worthwhile deal. One worthwhile point to note when working out the numbers is to take into account any cost of borrowing. What I mean, for example, is if you are releasing funds out of your own home, or borrowing from any other source for the deposit or refurbishment works, the cost of this borrowing needs to be taken into account when you work out your return.

I hope that you can now see clearly the basic, yet vital components to assessing whether a property is financially viable in the first place. I cannot emphasize this point enough. If you practice the formulas again and again on different examples, they soon become second nature, and you can apply them anywhere you look. Before too long, you become able to start 'spotting' potential deals even before you've worked them out!

The sustainability factor

Sustainability—this word has become very important to me in *every* aspect of my investment decisions over more recent years. The need for your property business to be sustainable has become even more crucial over recent years having witnessed countless people lose their existing portfolios, jobs and/or homes. I have discovered that there are many facets to this point which I would like to cover here. I consider this to really be such a critical factor in any successful property portfolio business that it warrants a good look at here. I will list the points I want to make to help you see it from a clear perspective. Here's what I mean by sustainability:

- ⌂ The deal will work in almost any market (and allow you to be flexible with the way it is configured if necessary).
- ⌂ The area you choose has a proven track record of steady or even growth without extremes of highs and lows compared to the national average.
- ⌂ The property will stand the test of time and be built and/or refurbished to last.
- ⌂ It will be environmentally friendly and meet all current and ideally future energy-saving standards (especially those to be implemented by the government in the Energy Act of 2018).
- ⌂ The income derived from the property will be ongoing and rental demand high.
- ⌂ The cash flow created from the property will more than cover any fluctuations in interest rates over the longer term.
- ⌂ Under ideal circumstances, if you have set the deal up correctly, you will be able to pull out most if not all of your own resources (initial seed capital) from any property when you refinance it so that you can continue to build your portfolio over many years. This is what I refer to as 'The Holy Grail' of property investment!
- ⌂ It will enable you to leave a legacy to your family.

If these factors are taken into consideration when building your business, you create sustainability in your portfolio over the longer term, ensuring you achieve what you had originally intended for the business.

The Holy Grail!

I felt that this statement needed a little more explanation. As touched on above, when you become a property investor, the major key to your success is to be able to buy a property below its market valuation and increase the value of that property, which will enable you to restructure that deal by refinancing it and re-leasing your own money back out. Thus buying for wholesale and selling/refinancing for retail. When working with a finite amount of capital, it is best for you to keep it as fluid as possible so that you can continue to invest and build your portfolio, should you desire. As an alternative, and if you have a large sum of money to work with, you may decide to keep the property 'unencumbered', which means have no mortgage or borrowings against it. Increasing its value will have just increased the level of return you achieve on that pot you leave in. When we really grasped this, it was a complete revelation. The first time we achieved it was on a 2 bedroom flat in Southsea in 2004. We bought the property for £93,000 and spent £3,500 on costs to buy and sell and £8,500 on the refurbishment. The total amount of funding was therefore £105,000. The property then valued up at £129,950. We had originally bought it to hold; however, we were keen to realise that sort of profit early on, so decided to sell for an offer of £127,000. At the time, that amount of profit (£22,000) was more than my annual earnings! You can see why it became such a discovery. If we had held the property, we would, at the time, have refinanced it to 85% LTV, meaning that the mortgage raised would have been £107,950—enough to pay us back entirely as well as £2,950 surplus cash out of the deal. We would have been left with a property with £19,050 of equity bringing in a rent of £625 which would have been enough to cover the mortgage and other expenses and a small amount of cash flow.

Letting and tenant management

This is a large topic to cover, so I will only really touch on the most relevant points. The process of letting and managing a property is essential to get right. There are a few options open to you. When we first started, we got to know some of the local letting agents and chose two to work with. We would instruct them to find a tenant for us, and then we took over the ongoing management. This is a great way to learn your business from the inside out and will give you a good view into what a good letting agent should actually be doing. With a good letting agent on your side, they will ensure (to the best of their knowledge) that you have a sound tenant. They will run the referencing process and credit checks and make sure that what the tenant says 'checks out'. With experience on their side, they will also have a good idea of gut feeling on a person when they walk through the door. You can of course choose to find a tenant yourself and go through the checks independently. We have done this at times and have found websites like www.gumtree.com and www.rentify.com invaluable to post up a free or low cost advert to market your property. We use a company called www.tenantverify.co.uk to run the referencing and credit checks through and meet the tenants ourselves. We have a professional inventory clerk in to draw up a condition report before the tenant moves in and produce our own tenancy agreements, a simple enough task.

The alternative is to have your property fully managed from the start. This is where the letting agent will find a tenant, collect the rent and also deal with the day-to-day running of the property. We have a mixture in our portfolio depending on how far away the property is located and whether we want to be involved or not. On the whole, apart from the occasional 'bad egg', we have fantastic tenants who look after our properties well. We give them a decent standard home to live in and have found that the vast majority respect that and treat it as if they owned it.

An important point to note: if any of your tenants ever slips into arrears or you notice the standard of the property slipping, act immediately. Have a good system in place to deal with such issues. The challenging situations we have encountered only got worse because we were sympathetic to their stories and gave them some leeway. When all is said and done, you are running a business, not a charity! Act professionally and courteously yet firmly and nip any problems in the bud. If worse comes to worst, it is best to work with a professional team of people to help you get the tenant out as efficiently and effectively as possible.

Managing your portfolio
The key to any smooth-running business is to systemise your operations, and this couldn't be truer than in a property business. Don't learn the hard way (as we did!) and have to back track and catch up with yourself. Learn to file and administrate as you go along—it makes life so much easier! I wish I had been taught back at the beginning how to manage admin and do accounts properly as it would have saved a lot of time having to put it all into order some way down the line.

Filing and administration
If you already operate a portfolio, or have even only purchased a single property before, you will know and have experienced that 'property breeds paperwork'! I don't know what the files do of a night, but the piles can just seem to keep getting bigger if you don't keep them under control—especially when you are into the realms of multiple property purchases.

Get organised and have a good filing system. All that needs to be are some box files and maybe a filing cabinet with drop files in. I categorise every element of each transaction into different headings and file away accordingly. The same goes for your computer. Make sure you make sense of the emails coming in and files which need to be kept properly for future reference.

It is always a good idea to keep a renewals spreadsheet detailing when important events need to happen such as GSC (Gas Safety Certificate), ESC (Electrical Safety Certificate), PAT tests (Portable Appliance Testing), insurance renewals, etc. as well as when fixed term mortgage interest rates come up for renewal and the like. If you are on top of these, you will be running your business responsibly and with the necessary due care and attention it deserves, and this will serve you well in the long-term.

Keeping a portfolio spreadsheet is also a great idea as you then have the vast majority of information about each property to hand at a glance. You can have details, such as the purchase price, current value, mortgage amount, mortgage interest rate, mortgage term, lender details, mortgage account number, repayment amounts, rent, expenses, net cash flow, etc., etc.

There are some very good property portfolio software managers you can purchase where you can input all this data and keep a close track on how everything is going. Initially though, what I have suggested here will suffice until you have built up the numbers and need something a little more professional.

Accounting

For many, accounting procedures can be a chore and create many a headache amongst us! However, if you again have a good system, which you keep up-to-date, this needn't be the case. A simple case of keeping receipts in a folder and going through them once a month, allocating relevant expenses to each property and inputting mortgage and rent payments is enough to keep on top of things. You can do this yourself or employ the services of a bookkeeper or accountant to do it for you. Whatever you do, keep details of all costs relating to the property, including purchase, legal fees, mortgage broker and valuation costs, refurbishment fees, travel expenses, etc., etc. Your accountant will know which expense will go against which form of taxable income. As a rule of thumb (and please check this out yourself as I am no tax specialist!), initial purchase costs normally go against any capital gain you make and any ongoing costs go against rental income received. Depending on the level of refurbishment you do, these expenses could fall in to either category. I would always advise seeking specialist tax advice as each individual's set of circumstances is different. The most important thing is to ensure that you submit accounts to the Inland Revenue, and ultimately they will decide how you are taxed on which income.

Rules and regulations

There really are a plethora of 'rules and regs' in this business—far too many to list here. You can research until the cows come home all the litigation around being a landlord and investor. I mean here to inform you rather than to scare you off as most of it is pretty straightforward once you get going and know what the basics are. The most important to get right are the following:

- Seek planning permission or building control consent from the local council for any building works, refurbishment works or alterations needed to ensure the job is done properly and within the law.
- Set up an HMO property properly to conform to all the correct levels of fire safety, regulation, licensing and having a FSC (Fire Safety Certificate—in addition to Gas and Electrical Safety Certificates)—renewable every two years—and amenities standards, etc.

- ⌂ Ensure that your property has a current EPC (Energy Performance Certificate) prior to letting or selling the property—to be done every ten years.
- ⌂ It is law to have a GSC (Gas Safety Certificate)—renewable every year—in place for any let property. It is also your responsibility to ensure the electrics are safe, and although this is not yet law at the time of writing this book, it is advisable to have an ESC (Electrical Safety Certificate) for each of your let properties too—needed every five years and every year on portable appliances.
- ⌂ Ensure the correct type of AST (Assured Shorthold Tenancy) agreement is in place at the beginning of each new tenancy.
- ⌂ Have a well-documented inventory at the start and end of each tenancy.
- ⌂ Make sure that a tenant's deposit is registered with a tenant's deposit protection scheme within two weeks of letting a property, such as the DPS (Deposit Protection Service), TDS (Tenancy Deposit Scheme) or similar.

As I said, there are many more things to consider, and it is advisable to register with one of the national landlords' schemes such as the NLA (National Landlords Association) or RLA (Residential Landlords Association) to keep up with current legislation as it is an area which is constantly being reviewed and changed. If something goes wrong with a property, ignorance is not an excuse. Being a responsible landlord is something I advocate to all my clients, and the learning doesn't stop after you've bought your first property—it is an ongoing process.

My Top Five 'Golden Rules' and 'Biggest Mistakes'

Here is a brief and to the point synopsis of what I consider to be the top five elements of successful as opposed to unsuccessful property investment. For further top tips, download your free copy of my eReport 'Golden Rules for Successful Property Investment – An Investor's Essential Guide' on my website www.whypropertyworks.co.uk.

Top Five 'Golden Rules'

1. *Know and understand why you are investing*

   I truly believe this to be the most critical element to your success. I urge you to remember this, as your initial reason and motivation may not be the real reason behind wanting to invest. I have covered this point in depth already.

2. *Get educated—properly!*

   A little bit of information is a dangerous thing in this industry. When you are talking about tens of thousands if not hundreds of thousands of pounds, making a decision based on sketchy if not plain bad information can work seriously against you.

3. *Property is a people business*

   Property investment is a people business—90% people, 10% property! If you think about it, every step along the process of purchasing, refurbishing, selling or letting and managing a property involves...people! Focus on how best you can help people in this business, and you will experience true success.

4. ***Do your due diligence and research before buying***
   This is an absolute must. Regardless of where the deal is coming from, you must perform your own research and due diligence before committing to buy any property.

5. ***Treat it like a business***
   This point includes many elements, from understanding the reason behind the purchase of each property, overestimating costs and underestimating values, buying wholesale and selling retail, knowing your numbers thoroughly and protecting the downside by having a minimum of two exit strategies for each purchase you make. These all constitute running a good portfolio business.

Top Five 'Biggest Mistakes'

1. ***Investing in the wrong area for your strategy/ requirements***
   As an example, this means when you buy a property as a cash flow investment expecting an immediate ROI through rental returns and ending up with the property either breaking even or, worse, costing you money each month instead. The property has therefore not met your objectives.

2. ***Buying deals listening solely to advice from others without doing your own research***
   Again, I have met too many people who have done this and suffered as a consequence. Remember, the only person who has your best interests at heart is you. Never just blindly trust someone else to know what

constitutes the best investment for you—you give your power away by doing this. Paying for the right guidance on how to do this properly, however, can save you and make you a fortune.

3. *Not understanding the numbers properly*
   I reiterate the point here that far too few people truly understand the financials of the property business. This includes how debt can work against you, how not accounting for depreciation can potentially jeopardise your portfolio, how interest rate fluctuations can affect you and how miscalculating the cost of borrowing (i.e., if you've raised a loan or increased your home mortgage to put down as a deposit) can actually put you into negative cash flow, etc.

4. *Not knowing when to buy...or when to sell*
   I have met many people who have tried to time the market 'just right' and therefore never bought anything. I have also worked with a number of people who try to 'hang on' to a property for dear life even when it is taking them down and just don't understand how or when to 'take a hit' if need be.

5. *Thinking that this business is 'easy' and that financial independence is just around the corner*
   Regardless of what you may hear, property is not a 'get rich quick' scheme and never will be. Certainly, there are people who have made a fortune from property, although this is generally over a long period of time and by someone having had quite a lot of experience. There will always be the very occasional 'exception to the

rule' but please, whilst building this up, in the meantime keep your day job!!

Of course, these are but my own personal opinions and should be taken as such. I do not profess to 'know it all' in this business. I am just getting my message out there. There are many, many more 'rules' or 'guidelines' you could follow; when you start off and during the course of investing, you will discover your own along the way. These are just a few to either get you off on the right foot or help you progress.

8. Buying a house is a BIG DEAL

→ Finding the right property ←

Buying a house
is a big deal

Searching for and finding
the right property

IF YOU HAVE EVER BOUGHT a house before, you will already know much about this process and understand what I am talking about within this chapter. As we know, buying and moving into a new home is one of the most stressful times in a person's life. When investing in a property, the process should, in theory, be much less emotional and stressful, but in reality, it can be just as much so. Whichever way you look at it, buying a property is a big deal. You are taking on a large commitment and responsibility, and this ought to be taken seriously. Of course, the more times you do it, the easier it does become and the more you take things in your stride, although you still need to treat each purchase with the respect it deserves. If you feel yourself becoming complacent, you need to be aware and not let your standards slip.

Where to look online

The vast majority of people these days start their search for property online. The internet is truly a phenomenal tool for helping you to analyse, research and run your due diligence whether purchasing a home or an investment. Below, I have listed some of the more useful websites in order for you to begin your search. I have not gone into detail here as this is a whole topic in itself; it's more to give you a flavour of what's out there.

> *Rightmove* – www.rightmove.co.uk – a fantastic website which sorts properties by location, property type, price range, number of bedrooms, for sale or rent, etc. I use this site for a lot of my due diligence, especially in a new area and to compare rental figures against purchase prices. The other version of this is www.property-bee.com, which is a version of Rightmove that can only be accessed via the Mozilla Firefox web browser. This site gives you a kind of 'back office' version of Rightmove in that it tells you also when properties were listed, whether they've had a price revision and any other useful information that is listed regarding any property in particular since going on to Rightmove—an extremely useful tool!

> *Zoopla* – www.zoopla.co.uk – this property search tool is similar to Rightmove with the addition of being able to find out previous sold prices as well as area statistics.

> *NetHousePrices* – www.nethouseprices.com – a fantastic tool for finding out what properties have sold for in the past as well as let prices. Great for being able to get 'real' values as opposed to 'on the market' values! This does, however, have limited history as records only go back to the late 1990's, so anything prior to this will not be listed.

Mouseprice – www.mouseprice.com – a great resource for all things property. Again, similar to those I have already listed, but each has its own unique qualities and useful bits which the others don't have. This site includes features such as area guide, 'heatmaps', price trends, price/earnings ratio, average current values, housing stock, most and least expensive streets, etc., etc. A tool well worth using.

Google Maps – maps.google.co.uk/maps? – here you can type in the postcode of a street where you are looking at a property and use the Street View facility to take a close look at the property you want to go and view. This way you can see what the street is like even before you decide to go there! I have heard of a few occasions where my clients have used this tool and found that 'deals' they have been given are actually in the middle of nowhere, in an industrial site or in a completely derelict condition! Just be aware that not all streets have the Street View service and that the data is now a few years old, so it's always best to go and actually see the property before putting an offer in! In case you don't have the postcode in order to search, you can always use the postcode finder on the Royal Mail site at www.royalmail.com/postcode-finder/ or Google the first part of the address and the postcode should come up somewhere. Google Earth is also handy to see an aerial view of a plot to spot any development potential.

Of course, there are a myriad other ways of sourcing property online, lead generating websites, Gumtree, property forums and even eBay! Use the web creatively, and you will find all sorts of different ways.

How to source offline

Although there are many ways of sourcing online, there are an equal number offline, too. Here are some of the best ways to source offline...

Estate Agents – this is by far the most traditional and popular route for people to search for properties offline. Some of the best deals come from estate agents (despite their reputation!), just bear in mind that it takes the right approach, dedication to building the relationship, being professional and always doing what you say you're going to do and not wasting their time before you really 'crack the code' of working with them in the way that's best for you.

Letting agents – believe it or not, you can occasionally source deals from letting agents. After all, they have numerous landlords on their books who potentially may, every now and again, like to offload their property/ies to another investor for a quick and pain-free sale.

Goldmine adverts – this is where you place an advert into a local paper or post a card in a newsagent window offering to 'Buy Houses For Cash' or other such attention-grabbing headlines. This can be effective, but you must have a good system in place to deal with the leads that come in as well as knowledge and experience of what to say and how to work with people who come to you. I have found that unless you have this down to a 'T', you could waste a lot of time and money.

Leafleting – a strategy whereby you put leaflets out in a designated area, again offering to buy houses as a private buyer. This strategy also takes tenacity, organisation and patience as well as knowledge of the local area and different exit strategy options.

Word of mouth – sometimes, there's nothing better than a good old-fashioned referral. Word of mouth referrals can often be well worth pursuing as it is direct person-to-person contact. I would include in this attending local Landlord Forums, which are often set up by the local council to keep landlords informed of changes in legislation, etc. These are good places to network and meet like-minded investors who may be thinking of selling or know someone who is.

Networking events – I am, to a large extent, in favour of networking events. I feel that they offer investors a good place to meet and mingle with other people who are also interested or already involved in property. There is normally a good level of experience in the room, and people are generally very helpful when asked. The downside is that there can also be a number of less scrupulous people who are just looking to sell you their not-so-fantastic 'deals', and this is where you need to be cautious. Knowing your own remit is crucial before depending on the opinions and 'advice' of others.

Sourcing agents and deal packagers

There are so many people who call themselves sourcing agents and deal packagers it is really hard, unless you're already a seasoned investor, to be able to find 'a diamond amongst the rocks'. The most important thing is to use your common sense, check them out (as I've already written about earlier) and do your own research to back-up what they are saying. I have provided a list of questions below for you to run past anyone who approaches you offering these types of services. Believe me, there are some very good people out there who do this, although in my experience it is a little like trying to find a needle in a haystack, so make sure you find someone who is right for you. This is a totally unregulated industry, and it is very much a 'buyer beware' scenario. I have heard too many horror stories to let this point go unmentioned.

Answers to the following points are what I would expect a person or company to provide me with before I would even consider working with them. They must be transparent about their business practices and fees, have a comprehensive contract that clearly defines what they do and what you're paying for, have a good track-record and provable examples, be prepared to show you examples of deals they have bought in for people and have excellent (and genuine!) client testimonials. Here is a list of questions to help you get started:

- How long have you been in trading as a sourcing company? (Search on Companies House)
- Do you source the properties yourselves, if not who do you use?
- How long have you used them and what is your relationship with them?
- What sort and amount of due diligence do you carry out?
- What are your fees and when do you get paid?
- Are you registered with any professional bodies?
- How are deals bought by investors—what structure do you use?
- At what level do you bring the properties in—e.g., % below market value?
- Do you provide a full schedule of works needed and a breakdown of costs?

- ⌂ Are there independent entry and exit RICS valuations provided?
- ⌂ Do you have local knowledge of the areas where properties are sourced?
- ⌂ What are your terms and conditions?
- ⌂ What is your refund policy?
- ⌂ Do you have public indemnity insurance?
- ⌂ Do you provide a project management service for refurbishment?
- ⌂ Do you provide a lettings service?

Different ways of financing

There are various ways of purchasing a property, some more creative than others. I must state at this point that I do not advocate the use of any 'no money down' structures. There has been much discussion about these types of ventures in the past, and to some extent there is still. Whilst there may have been a possibility of doing this in times gone by, it is, in my opinion, not legal now. The closest you could get now to 'no money down' now is by borrowing funds from someone else to put down on the property and/or raising finance another way, therefore technically meaning that you have put none of your own funds in. Be aware that if you are looking to raise a mortgage on the property either at the purchase or refinance stage, many lenders do not look particularly favourably on this type of arrangement (with the exception possibly being to use a bona fide bridging company). Anything other than this with fancy, roundabout structures I would leave well alone.

Buying with a deposit and raising a mortgage

Buying a house with a deposit and raising a mortgage is the most popular way of buying. It is one of the most conventional routes for people and allows you to leverage the money you are putting in yourself. This enables you to buy a property for far more value than you are able to raise yourself. The most important element in this option is to find yourself a good mortgage broker. This person will be crucial in providing you with the best mortgage product for your needs. It is no use just going for the lowest interest rate if the deal locks you in for three years and has a crucifying early redemption charge when your intention is to 'flip' the property! This is where a good mortgage broker can find you a 'best fit' product and look at your overall objectives, including future purchases. You will need to decide between fixed rate and fixed term, repayment or interest-only, variable or capped products. It is a suggestion that you find a broker who invests themselves so that they understand things from your perspective, not just from the amount of commission they are likely to make! It is better to pay a fee to a broker if they are worth their salt rather than opting for a 'free' broker if they are not going to offer you the best advice in the end.

Buying for cash

This is obviously pretty self-explanatory; however, I will give reasons here why it can be beneficial to buy a property for cash.

It makes for a great bargaining tool. Estate agents and vendors alike love it when there is a buyer in a strong position to buy as a sale can normally proceed (subject to contract) fairly swiftly and hopefully without too many complications!

Having cash in the bank can mean that you are able to negotiate a really good discount based on the fact that you can proceed straight away if a vendor needs to sell quickly.

Without having to involve a lender, this can mean that if you wish to refinance a property after six months (and in some cases sooner), there is no previous history in a credit file, and if you can prove that you have significantly improved the property, it may make it easier to justify an increase in the value and therefore pull your money back out (if structured correctly).

The time to purchase can be significantly less, sometimes even only a few days if you take out certain indemnity insurance policies to cover you for different eventualities, therefore putting you massively ahead of the competition. This is heavily down to your conveyancing solicitor's opinion and efficiency too.

Buying with a JV (Joint Venture) partner

It is important to note that the law has changed since January 2014 around the topic of Joint Venture partnerships. It is wise to keep yourself informed of the latest rules and regulations which surround this aspect. For more information, visit the FCA (Financial Conduct Authority) website—www.fca.org.uk. This option can work really well for those with limited funds themselves. Bear in mind that a lot will depend on your ability to source and structure deals in a way that works for all parties concerned. This is basically where you borrow money from someone to fund a project which you will be responsible for and in which they will receive a return on their investment. You are devoting time, and they are devoting resources. I would like to emphasize, however, that if you are putting none of your own money in, a JV partner will question where your risk element is. If the deal was to go pear-shaped, you could just walk away leaving them high and dry. I find it is always best to commit some of your own resources if you can, to show that you are committed.

This method can be an incredibly powerful way of pooling resources in order to make a deal work which may otherwise not have happened. It is vital to discuss all relevant business factors up front so that you know, for example, how you will split the profits, who has responsibility for what, who will own the property and in what proportion and what would happen if things do not go according to plan. You must then have this drawn up in a clear legal agreement, which is normally done through a solicitor.

Bridging finance

In my opinion, bridging finance is my least favourite way to finance the purchase of a property. In case you are not familiar with this method of finance, a 'bridging loan' is just like taking out any other type of loan, although over a generally much shorter period of time and for significantly higher costs. For example, if you were looking to borrow £25,000 over seven months to fund the deposit and purchase costs of a property, you will most likely have to pay an 'entry fee' of anywhere from £500+, 1.25%+ interest per month and a 'closing fee' of anywhere above £500+ (occasionally lower, but often much higher than these figures). For the privilege of borrowing this amount over seven months, you are therefore looking at repaying a minimum of £3,188 in bridging costs to enable you to do this.

The reason therefore that I am not a great advocate of this form of funding is that there is too much risk factor. There are too many 'what if...?' scenarios which could crop up and cause you stress and the added worry of having to pay more than you bargained for. Taking out a bridging loan is not for the faint-hearted (nor for the novice in my view) and should only be done when all the risk factors have been weighed up and calculated in. You must consider the likely end value of the project incredibly carefully (and pessimistically, just in case!), know that you'll be able to raise mortgage finance when it comes time to do this, be realistic on timescales for any refurbishment work or how putting a tenant in may affect the end price, etc., etc. If you are willing to take these chances and weigh up the numbers extremely carefully, then it can be a good solution under certain circumstances. Remember, due diligence is the absolute key here.

Negotiation

The art of purchasing a property which really makes sense in your portfolio has a lot to do with how well you can negotiate and bring the deal in for the right amount to begin with. Of course, there are plenty of tips and tricks to negotiation, and you need to develop your own 'style'. What works best for one person may be disastrous for another. The most important thing to remember is to be yourself. Trying to pretend you're someone or something you are not will be 'read' subconsciously by the agent or vendor you are dealing with and will often result in rejection at the first hurdle. Knowing how to talk to people and understand what *they* want is by far the best initial route. After all, if you are not aligning what they need or would like to achieve from the deal with what you have to offer, there will be a mismatch time after time. Making sure you are going to see the right type of project for your needs initially is a good starting point so that you do not waste your time or anyone else's. Finding something to make a compliment about will always go down well with a vendor (when dealing directly), even if the place is a pit! Even saying that the kitchen is a good size or making a nice comment about a family photo can be the start of gaining rapport and making the vendor open to your feedback.

There are so many comments I could write to help, I will be writing another tips book on this very subject. Keep up to date with regular news and more insights and extra bonuses on my website www.whypropertyworks.co.uk. Be aware that the ne-gotiation process can be anything from immediate agreement to months of to-ing and fro-ing before an agreement is reached.

Surveys

When buying a house, it is highly advisable that you have a survey done. Without one, you really are 'buying blind', and even then, it depends on the type of survey you instruct and what purpose it is for. I won't go into too much detail here other than to give you a glimpse of what the different types are. It is very much up to personal choice as to which survey you opt for when buying, but at least this gives you an idea of what they are.

Basic valuation

This is a very basic type of survey normally instructed by the lender you are negotiating your mortgage with. It essentially covers the risk element of the mortgage company to make sure that they are lending against a 'good risk' and that the building isn't going to fall down any time soon! It will only be a couple of pages long and will not go into detail about anything except major structural issues, damp (although in some cases not even this) and will list basic works needed and a very rough estimate of the costs of works. It will give you a value at time of purchase and may give you an estimated end value once works have been completed (and only if works are required). This type of survey should be instructed only if you are very confident that the property is in good, sound, basic order at least.

Homebuyer report

If you instruct a Homebuyer report, you will be pretty well informed as to the state of the property. Of course, it is more ex-pensive to purchase but in some cases can be well worth it. The report is normally around 25 pages long and uses a traffic light coding system to indicate the immediacy of any works needed. A green rating will indicate that no repair is needed, an amber rating is for remedial works needed, i.e., those which need attention but are not serious in nature, and of course a red rating indicating that immediate work is required to repair, replace or investigate further to bring that element up to standard.

There are a number of sections to this report detailing everything from energy efficiency to potential risks, such as dangers to small children, flooding, asbestos, etc., and will also state the valuer's opinion on the agreed purchase price of the property.

Building survey

This, of course, is the top type of survey you can have and is generally recommended for properties which are 75 years or older, are of unusual construction or have had a number of alterations or extensions. You can expect, of course, a very thorough and detailed report of findings about the property, and the surveyor will list all major and minor faults. The report is very long and will list all the findings as well as all recommended specialist investigations required. You may note here that the list may be fairly exhaustive of things that need doing and an estimate of works will be included too. The surveyor has to note the worst case scenarios within the report and will over-estimate costs just to cover themselves for any unforeseen eventuality. As this process is much more in-depth, you may have to wait up to two weeks to receive your copy.

The conveyancing process

Often what is referred to as a time-consuming and complicated process in many peoples' view, conveyancing is a really important part of the property purchasing equation. If this is not done correctly by a competent solicitor, you could be leaving yourself open to potentially uncovering a can of worms later on down the line, so it is imperative that you choose the right solicitor to take care of this for you. I have discovered that there are many different standards of conveyancing solicitor, so again, do your due diligence in choosing the best one.

How long is a piece of string?

By far the most frustrating part of buying a property can be taken up with the legal process. Remember that you are working with two sets of solicitors (yours and the vendor's) and that often their practices and procedures can be wildly varied! You may have the most competent solicitor in the land, and yet the vendor's solicitor could turn out to be going backwards—or so it may feel! This process is very much 'solicitor-dependent' so don't be surprised that what should be a four-week process may actually end up taking a few months on occasions.

When things don't go according to plan, either as a result of what the searches on a property have thrown up or that the solicitors you are working with insist (even in this age of super high-tech communication!) on working with 'snail mail' between each other and you, or any other incidence crops up, it is essential that you remain calm and composed and learn to just 'go with the flow'. If you have agreed to purchase within a certain set time-scale, you must of course do everything you possibly can to ensure this happens smoothly and make sure that all parties are aware of the situation and that they are 'on the same page' as you when it comes to paperwork and efficiency.

Things you can do to speed up the process include keeping in regular contact with your estate agent (or vendor), your broker (if you are using one) and your solicitor to make sure that everyone is pushing the sale through at the appropriate pace. Make sure that you get any forms requiring your attention or signature returned promptly and correctly and any payments you are required to make are done on time. If you are able to have contact with the vendor, keep in touch with them too to see how they are getting on with things at regular intervals.

A golden rule to remember when purchasing property is to 'expect the unexpected'! Very few purchases or sales that I have experienced or witnessed have been totally plain sailing and hassle-free, so keeping your cool if and when a situation arises is a good idea. You may also find yourself in a 'chain' of sales, which, of course, adds to the equation when factoring in all those other transactions.

The order of events

There are essentially three main stages to the conveyancing process, and I have briefly outlined them as follows:

1. *Stage 1* – Before exchange of contracts
    Your solicitor will contact the seller's solicitor who will then receive and negotiate the draft contract. This will include yours and the seller's details and price agreed, etc. Your solicitor will then make pre-contract enquiries and should send you a property information form for you to check the details contained therein. Your solicitor will then apply to the local council for local searches, which includes information about plans for the area, planning permission on empty or run-down land or properties in the vicinity, environmental issues (including flood risk), etc., as well as a list of enquiries to the seller's solicitor to include information about any disputes, boundary issues, rights of way, covenants,

services, guarantees, list of contents included in the sale, etc. Further searches may be required depending on the area in which you are purchasing, and these may include commons searches or coal-mining searches for example. If the property is leasehold, then questions will be sent to the managing agent to find out who the freeholder is, whether the service charge and ground rent payments are up-to-date and what works are needed in the near future. The contract is then negotiated and agreed and a completion date is set. If you are getting a mortgage, then you will be issued with a formal mortgage offer at this stage, and your solicitor will send you a mortgage deed to sign.

2. *Stage 2* – Exchange of contracts
   Once you and your solicitor are satisfied that everything is in order, you will sign a copy of the contract, which is then passed to the seller and likewise they will sign a copy, which is passed to you. Contracts are exchanged (normally by the two solicitors), and you are both legally bound to follow through with the transaction. You are also required to hand over a deposit (normally 10% of the purchase price) which is non-refundable if you pull out of the sale. Your solicitor will then draw up a transfer document which is sent to the seller's solicitor. This document transfers the title of the property from the seller to the buyer. The next step is for your solicitor to organise the finalisation and signing of your mortgage documents and arrange for the monies to be in place for completion of the sale. Final searches and enquiries are made at this point to ensure there are no charges relating to the property (e.g., undisclosed mortgages or

disputes), and you will be required to pay stamp duty (if needed) and Land Registry fees.

3. **Stage 3** – Completion
Hooray!! You've finally made it here, and after paying the balance owed to the seller (either in cash or by mortgage), you can pick up the keys to the property. The seller is obliged to move out, and you gain control of the property. In due course, you will be sent the transfer document and title deeds, and you will be asked to pay any full monies owed to the solicitor, etc. At this point, your solicitor has a few final matters to attend to, namely informing (where relevant) your mortgage company, life insurance company and freeholder that the sale has completed. Registration of the transfer of ownership will also take place at the Land Registry, who will send out the title deeds to your lender, who keeps them until you either sell the property or pay off the mortgage. They will pay the Stamp Duty owed and send you a statement of completion including a summary of financial transactions.

An important point to remember is that you become legally liable for the property from the moment you exchange contracts, meaning that you must insure the property from this point. If you intend to let the property, you must purchase landlords' insurance, which covers the building (if freehold), the contents (if you choose) and public liability. If the property will be undergoing refurbishment, you must inform the insurance company as it will be put under a different type of 'risk' cover whilst this is happening. Once you complete, you must inform the relevant local council regarding council tax (you will sometimes have

6–12 months exemption if a property is undergoing refurbishment or is vacant and unfurnished) as well as the utilities. It is worth noting here that when you are buying property to hold and rent out for the longer term, if you personally move house in the meantime, you must inform the Land Registry that you have done this. If you do not, they have no record of where you are, and I have heard horror stories (believe it or not!) of people copying identities and selling or remortgaging other people's houses without them ever knowing, just because the Land Registry has no record of the true owner's current address!! The moral of the story here is to keep your records up-to-date.

The renovation and refurbishment process

Not necessarily every house you purchase will need renovating and refurbishing; however, if you are looking to add value to the property yourself, it inevitably will to some degree or other. Whether you are looking to buy and hold property for the long-term or do a quick trade, you need to think carefully about what level of works will need doing and, more importantly, who is going to do them. A vital aspect to cover is that of doing any works needed to Building Control standards or obtaining the correct Planning Permission from the local authority the property is located. If you are at all unsure about what the building requirements are, you must seek the advice of the Planning/Building Control officers from the local council. If you do not follow their guidance when refurbishing a project, you could be in breach of the law and jeopardise the health and safety and legal aspects of what you are doing, especially when you ever come to refinance or sell the property. If your refurbishment falls within needing consent, you (or your builder/project manager) must ensure you fill out the correct paperwork and arrange site visits with the relevant people to inspect your property as you go along to make sure it is 'signed off' at the end so you can prove you have fulfilled their requirements.

Assessing costs correctly

When working out the costs of refurbishment works on a property, there are certain aspects you must take into consideration well before you make an offer to purchase. If you are new to investing, you really must do your homework and research how much different aspects of the work will cost you. This will be very much area-dependent as the costs to renovate a property in Manchester will be very different to London for example. Labour costs as well as materials, fixtures and fittings will all be priced differently according to where you live in the country. You must become a local 'expert' in your pricing, or find a local and knowledgeable person whom you can trust to know on your behalf.

When I assess a property for works, I always make a full list of what needs to be done, and knowing my area, I set about 'pricing the job'. If I'm not certain of the costs of a particular aspect, I will call local trades people in that field and ask. For example, the cost of replacing a roof can vary massively, so I ring around 3–4 roofing companies to pick their brains for a rough estimate and go from there. I will always overestimate the prices as well as underestimate the end value so that even in the worst case scenario, if the property stacks up, I can be sure it will work out even better if the best case scenario plays out.

Remember, even though these are direct costs associated with the refurbishment itself, if you are borrowing money to enable you to refurbish the property, the cost of these borrowings must be taken into account too for the duration of the project or until the time to refinance happens.

How to find the right builder

In my experience, you can't beat a good referral. Word-of-mouth recommendation is, to me, by far the best way of finding a good person to work with. This isn't to say that you couldn't strike lucky by finding someone from the Yellow Pages, but if you can, ask for recommended people. If I'm working in a new area, the first place I ask is at the local letting agents as they will have their favoured tradespeople, and if they are hoping to do business with you once the property is up and running, they should be pretty forthcoming with builder names. I will also ask agents whether they invest themselves and ask for personal recommendations if they've used someone in the area. Just a quick word of warning, there are some agents who get paid a commission from builders for them to recommend them, so always follow this up and make sure you're not being 'taken for a ride' and paying over the odds. Another avenue is to go through the 'Checkatrade' website—www.checkatrade.com—where you can find recommended people online. I tend to go for companies or people who have a good long(ish) term track record on there with excellent feedback from their customers.

The next step is to arrange to meet them at the property and ask them to assess the works needed. You must have a really good idea of what needs doing yourself so that you're not just being told by them. Notice how they are with you; are they friendly, professional, courteous, etc.? Can they provide testimonials and evidence of previous work, or even better, if it's a large-scale project, are you able to go and see some of their previous work? Ask how long they have been trading, how long they've been in the area, are they a member of a professional body (although this doesn't necessarily guarantee standards), do they have provable proper insurance and so on to really get a feel for whether you could work with them. Remember, you are going to have potentially quite a lot of contact with this person so you've got to know if you can work with them and, more importantly, trust them. Again, this decision will be based very much on gut feel. You also need to find out what their time-scales are in relation to when you are likely to complete on the property. It's no good if a builder has no availability for three months if you're completing in two weeks, so make sure you get your builders to quote right near the beginning of the purchasing process once you're set on a property.

Once you've had several quotes in from 3–4 builders, it's time to decide who you'll go for. After assessing all the above points, you will choose who to work with. Remember, there is no harm in negotiating on the price compared to the quotes you have in (as long as they're all for the same work!) but remember that the builder needs to make a living as well as some profit, otherwise they are unlikely to work with you again. A fair deal all-round is what you're after.

You need to obtain a proper schedule of works to include the details of all the works that will be carried out at the property. This, as I have experienced, can be quite tricky with some of the, shall I say, more senior generation of builders. They are fantastic at their work but can be hopeless at technology and business and therefore can't always get it together to send you a proper breakdown other than tell you what they'll do! I have found this difficult in the past on occasions as my gut feeling told me to work with one particular person who happened to fall into this category and so I went with a younger person who could, and it ended up that I should have trusted my gut feeling! The lesson is that there is no hard and fast rule particularly, but since you are in business, you really should treat it as such and, wherever possible, make sure the people you are working with are too.

After your schedule of works has been arranged, you then need to agree on a fixed price (not a day rate as this can work out far more expensive!) and a schedule for when you'll make the stage payments to the builder. Whatever you work out with them, always hold back the final 10% until you are completely happy with their workmanship. Agree on a time-frame that the project will take and any penalty charges that will be incurred if the job has not been completed by this time (if appropriate).

Project management

From the outset, you need to decide whether you will personally be involved in the day-to-day project management of the refurbishment, or whether you will hire in the services of a competent and qualified person to do the job for you. Much of this decision will depend on the logistical side of things. If you live close by and have time to pop across to keep an eye on everything as well as have the confidence and temperament to keep the builders 'on their toes', know what level of finish you expect and can communicate this, then I would advocate you taking on this responsibility. If, however, you are less experienced, or live much further away from your project, I would wholeheartedly recommend using the services of a project manager. When you are bringing a building back to life, it is crucial that the all-important details are taken care of and the standard of work is consistent throughout the build. Whatever you decide and depending on the complexity of the project, you may need to work closely with the building control team in the building regulations department of the local council and possibly even the planners if you are changing the structure of the building. They will keep an eye on what goes on and will sign the project off at the end—crucial when you come to sell at any point.

You need to ask yourself whether you have what it takes to do the job justice as well as the time involvement it will take to keep the project on track. You must consider how much work is needed and the order of that work to be done. You should be able to rely quite well on the builder to know the order of events if they're experienced, but this still shouldn't detract from you knowing what is going on when. If you do decide to hire in a professional project manager, make sure you take account of the fees they will charge and also what they will bring to the table in terms of experience and the potential end value of a job done properly. They may just be worth their weight in gold!

9. Getting it RIGHT isn't always EASY
→ A reality check ←

Getting it right isn't always easy!

A reality check

WHEN YOU FIRST GET INVOLVED in the world of property investing, you may have an idyllic picture of how it's going to be and that everything will just slot into place and the dream will just 'build itself' as a result of your actions. This is the image some property investment companies/gurus would have you believe so that they can sell the idea easily to you. When you find out for yourself what is really involved, you soon realise all may not be as it first appeared to be...

The whole process

When you start out in property, you may not have actually considered that you are in fact getting involved in a business, rather than just an investment. There is a complete set of processes that make up the whole package, and it is not to be undertaken lightly. Have you considered all the different factors that make up a successful property business and decided which ones you'll take on and which you'll delegate? If you're anything like myself and the vast majority of people I have worked with, you will take the DIY approach to begin with until you realise that there's just too much to do all by yourself! I remember the days when we did almost everything and were flat-out every waking moment sourcing, purchasing, refurbishing or letting, and it took its toll. Paperwork would mount up, and we didn't have the proper systems in place. We'd be stressed about co-ordinating projects and budgets and also be 'getting our hands dirty' on the refurbishments themselves (...oh, the heady days of camping out on a living room floor of the latest purchase, paintbrush in one hand, scrubbing brush in the other, exhausted after a weekend's work!!). We were not alone in realising the reality was very different to the initial dream.

Treading the streets

Here I mean the physical research, viewings, driving round to assess an area, meeting agents, etc. It takes a lot of time and energy to actually get out there and do it. During the first couple of years, we spent almost every evening and weekend actually implementing what we had learned and going out to find deals. It took time to build rapport and relationships with key people and to learn how to interact with people correctly and professionally. The times we got it 'wrong' were the most painful, yet the most educational! It most certainly was not *easy*. Having said that, it was ultimately very satisfying when you had got the job done, but I don't think either of us realised just what we were getting ourselves into. We literally had to build everything up around other time commitments, including work, family, friends, etc. and didn't really have much of a 'life' whilst going through this process. I guess what I mean here is that if you choose the DIY route, you will have to make a lot of sacrifices along the way, although if you're passionate enough about it and truly enjoy it, it is worth it.

You have to learn to take rejection

There's one thing you'll get very used to when embarking on property and that is to learn to take rejection! By this, I mean there are different types of rejection you may face, which can make it hard at times. Initially, when you mention what you are doing to friends and family, they may think you are completely barking mad! In my experience (and many of my clients), family members and friends can be the most negative and progress-stopping bunch of people you could ever hope to meet when it comes to doing something 'different'. Certainly, when I first started, I faced many a naysayer and people warning me of the risks and what did I think I was doing, me, a musician, in property?!?! Whilst there are indeed many who are willing to give you an 'opinion' on the property market and investing, are you really willing to listen to those who have no idea and no experience of doing so? I have also heard reports of people having the fear of God struck into them by horror stories told by well-meaning people who themselves may have experienced a tough time in the property market. I soon learned, however, to live by the motto 'whatever someone else says about or to me is actually about themselves' and this got me through. The importance of having the right mentor to guide you through this is imperative to your success. At this point, I would like to stress that I have always had the wonderful support of my parents who were always there for me and actually encouraged and supported us in what we were doing. They saw us through quite a rollercoaster journey and they were always there, so I'd like to publicly thank them for this.

Rejection also comes when you are looking for the perfect deal that 'fits'. As any experienced investor will tell you, it can take a long time before you find something which really works for you. You may have to 'kiss a lot of frogs before you find your prince' in this sense, and it can be very frustrating when all you are doing is in effect 'rejecting' all those property details which just don't stack up in order to find 'the one'. However, if you see each of your rejections as one step closer to finding the right property, this is a much healthier attitude and you won't feel as bogged down by the process.

Offers, offers, offers...you will almost certainly have to make a large number of offers once you have narrowed down the search to then have one eventually accepted which works for you. You have to develop tenacity in this game and be persistent with the number and types of deals you are negotiating on. It really can be worth it, but just ensure this is the case by working out your ROTI (remember...your Return On Time Invested) and see how much this deal will make you compared to the amount of time you have actually put in. It may be helpful to keep a diary note of the number of hours you spend doing research, viewings, negotiations, project co-ordination, etc., etc. for each deal that comes off against the return you *actually* make once the deal has completely finalised just so you know whether it has in actual fact all been worth it. I have had to do a serious reality check with several clients in the past on deals they found by themselves as against the time involvement they had put in only to find out they'd actually lost money through the whole process. It is painful but necessary if you are to get this business right.

Prior bad experiences

It may be that your property investment experience has been tainted by a previous negative experience, which you are finding hard to overcome. You may have tried the DIY approach before with little or no experience and have fallen into the type of situation I have just mentioned above. This goes something along the lines of 'I don't need help, I can do this myself and save money by educating myself', which is normally followed by a little internet research on 'how to buy investment property' whereby you scan through masses of information looking for the 'golden nuggets' which will ensure your success. This may even lead to you attending a couple of low-cost or free evening or day events where you are taught the theory and very little else and then decide to go it alone. You end up buying a property, which you don't really know about, for the wrong price (i.e., paying too much!), which then turns into the proverbial 'money pit' where you encounter problem after problem and costs spiral out of control at which point you are tearing your hair out and wishing you'd never even begun, sitting in a heap on the floor after a very long day of trying to 'sort it all out'!! Phew!

Another common circumstance I encounter is where a client has bought a property at the top of the market which has then been subject to the market crash of recent times thus resulting in losing a heap of equity and in fact ending up in negative equity. This means that they cannot afford to sell the property as it will not make enough to pay off the debt, and they are therefore stuck with it. The other factor which has a massive impact on their purchase is the fact that it is losing money on a monthly basis as the rental figures they were promised have never been achieved. They now find themselves in a downward spiral of cash being taken out of their pocket each month as well as the burden of the negative equity.

The other very sad and unfortunately all-too-often heard story is where people have literally been ripped off. There are, disappointingly, so many accounts I have been told where someone has been scammed out of reservation fees or deposits by companies which—to all intents and purposes—seemed legitimate. These are companies which are set up with the sole intention of conning people out of large sums of money. As I have covered in another chapter, it is a 'buyer beware' business, and you must do your own thorough research before handing any money over.

There are other stories of BMV companies not having delivered what was expected. In one case, my client had put down a reservation fee on a property sent to her by a company to which she had signed up. Fortunately, she had the good sense to run a lot of her own research and due diligence rather than just taking their word for it and discovered that the property was in the middle of nowhere, decidedly run-down and had estimated the value to be about £30K as opposed to the £70K the company said it was worth! The deal was that she would buy the property at 25% below the RICS value, therefore 75% of £70K being £52,500. When the independent RICS survey was carried out by a valuer she instructed, the property was in fact found to be worth only the £30K she had estimated. The company still, to this day, has not paid her back the reservation fee.

If you think this is bad, another client of mine bought a property literally from an email sent to him from...yes, you guessed it...another BMV deal company!!! After receiving the email, he bought the property 'blind' (meaning he didn't actually go and view it) and on trust. OK—so it was crazy for him to have even thought about doing this, but I know there are plenty of people who have been sucked in by these tactics. In short, the property was bought by him at £55K with a very dubious 'No Money Down' structure (of which he had NO clue how it was arranged) and supposedly valued at £70K. He spent a further £4K on the 'refurb' and paid out a sourcing and purchase fee of around £5K. The property was then let to a string of bad tenants who either trashed the place, failed to pay rent or even used it as a drugs den! I finally said, 'Enough's enough—you have to face facts and deal with this!' So he went down to the property with a colleague of mine who helped him out, only to discover that the original refurbishment money had never been used to refurbish it and in fact it needed another £12K to bring it back up to anywhere near a decent standard to live in, and even then it would only just be worth the £55K he had actually spent buying it! You can imagine then that there are some people for whom property has been an incredibly bad experience and who may have lost all confidence in ever buying again. I'm here to say that it is possible to recover from experiences such as these—it will take time and patience, but it can be done. Often, a huge lesson at the beginning of your investing career kicks you into 'let's get real' mode and prevents you from further unnecessary pain by vowing to turn things around and do the job properly next time!

The biggest hurdle...is YOU!

Whilst there is a strong case for blaming others for your mistakes and therefore avoiding taking responsibility, it's really about taking stock of what experiences you may have encountered in the past and moving on from them. If you are 'stuck' in the mix of much of what I spoke about in the 'Cut the C**p' chapter, then you will forever be making excuses for not having achieved what you'd expected to.

True success in property investment (and in fact in life in general I have found!) is to get over YOU!

The majority never even get going

The very fact that you are still here reading at this point shows that you potentially have what it takes to be a great investor or are already doing a pretty good job. Considering you are willing to look at it from a different perspective than the norm demonstrates that you are no ordinary person. Remember when I mentioned that 95% of people do nothing or very little with the information they learn? If you were to take action on what has been said in this book, you would be the exception rather than the rule. You do have to do some real soul-searching to find out whether it is truly right for you, though hopefully this book has been of some help to sort this out for you.

As a small reminder, if you find yourself procrastinating about this course of action, it is your subconscious telling you something. Also, if the 'analysis paralysis' mentality has got the better of you, remember that 'you don't have to get it right, you just have to get it going'. Trying to be a perfectionist in this business will get you nowhere fast, and one day you will just have to go for it with the best support and guidance behind you and make it happen. If you love it, you will find that this will keep you going and spur you on. The fact that the majority never even get going proves that property investment is not for everyone; just like any other occupation or subject is not for everyone. You just have to figure out if it *is* for you.

Negative self-talk

If, just like the rest of us, you suffer from the occasional bout of 'negative self-talk' and worry, firstly, know that it is completely normal and you are not the only one! If you find yourself worrying all of a sudden about mortgage interest rates rising or the current deal you have falling through or thinking about whether the builder is going to do the work properly or is your tenant going to trash the place or any other myriad thoughts you could have about property, then please STOP! The most important thing at this point is to then become aware of the thoughts that you may be having and just listen to them. I know this sounds a bit strange, but when you become aware of them and pay them some attention, they have a funny habit of vanishing. Bringing your *conscious* attention to your thoughts will stop the *unconscious* running of them and therefore let them ebb away without you having to 'try'. It's a bit like weeding a garden or finding a virus running on your computer and then dealing with it.

The next step is to just let it go. You may have come across the phrase of 'where focus goes, energy flows'. In this sense, you cannot pay attention to two thoughts at the same time, so if you stop having thoughts about one thing and instead focus on another, then the original disappears. It's like then planting a lovely flower in the place of the weed or uploading new software to protect from viruses, for example. One motto I live by now (as I used to be a real worry-pot!) is 'worry is like a rocking chair— it gives you something to do but never gets you anywhere!' by Erma Bombeck. So let go of that which is worrying you and instead focus on the task in hand and know you can deal with anything that crops up along the way. You will probably find that things just run smoother from this perspective.

The message here is to stop beating yourself up for any and every little thing. We are our own worst enemies when we do this.

Instead have confidence and self-belief

Confidence and self-belief come from a place of certainty. Certainty comes from a place of clarity and knowing. Knowing takes time and experience to gain, and this only happens through practice, patience and listening to your instincts.

I most definitely was not in any way, shape or form confident or certain when I first started investing in earnest. It has taken me many years to develop this, and I guess the fact that I've been tenacious and just 'got on with it' and learnt from all my experiences along the way has put me in the position I speak from now. I really do believe in myself now and what I am doing, and all I can tell you is 'it feels great!' This is ultimately what I want for you in whatever you choose to do. It is the number one goal I have when I work with my clients to have them feel this way and enjoy the journey.

The key is to celebrate the 'little wins'

For every small step you take towards achieving what you want from property, you must pat yourself on the back and say, 'Well done; I've done a good job'. You may have supporters along the way who will also encourage you and nurture your passion for this business, but it is you yourself who must keep the fire burning on a daily basis—particularly when you are first starting out. If you pick up the phone and make a good contact for your business, if you really learn how to run the numbers properly or get an offer accepted on a property for the first time, these are all 'little wins' which need to be savoured and enjoyed. You will discover that this is what the process is actually all about, and the 'bigger wins' will happen naturally as a result of an accumulation of the little wins.

Every now and again, reward yourself as an acknowledgement for having worked towards your goals. There is really no point whatsoever in being frustrated, frantic, stressed out and miserable on the way to building your portfolio as you will ultimately then end up hating the business. The more joyful and fun you make the experience, the better. After all, each step is significant and builds up to the bigger things happening. How often do we ever acknowledge our achievements and stop to 'smell the roses' as it were? All too infrequently in this fast-paced life we lead. Take the time to nurture and enjoy yourself on this path too.

10. WHAT IT REALLY TAKES

→Know your goals
& objectives ←

What it really takes

Know your goals and objectives

DURING THIS CHAPTER, YOU WILL read a round-up of what I consider to be all the most important points to owning and running a successful property business. Many of the points will have been raised before and a few will be new ideas to add to the melting pot. In reiterating some things, I am hoping they will really resonate with you now and 'sit right' as it were.

The WHY factor revisited

As suggested before, this, above anything else, will be what keeps you on track and focussed. It will be what enables you to get out of bed in the mornings and plough on regardless of any situation, in the firm knowledge that you are doing what's best for YOU. As soon as I found my why, it is what took my business to a whole other level, bringing meaning to every aspect of what I did and a clarity which I really hadn't been aware of before. In case you are wondering, my why is to inspire other people to be true to themselves by being true to myself in the process. I focus on capturing the essence of what life is all about—peace, love and joy and helping others experience the same. When you bring these elements to the fore, the world really is a better place...

Have a clear direction
Knowing exactly what it is that you want to achieve through property investment is one of the biggest factors of it actually happening. This sounds obvious, though for some it can be incredibly hard to pinpoint. The clearer you are, the more certainty you will feel and you won't help but to make positive moves in that direction. By keeping focussed and sticking to your chosen strategy (as long as you have researched that you can do it!), you will make it happen. If you learn to take it one step at a time, you will slowly and steadily find a rhythm. Don't be 'in a hurry', just take the necessary actions needed in order to start and continue the wheel in motion; momentum will gather of its own accord.

Making a proper investment plan is a great way of having this level of clarity. Knowing where you're at right now and how and when you're going to reach your targets will give your goals tangibility and help make the process more 'real' rather than just a 'nice dream'. It will also show you exactly what it's going to take to make it come about! By having a clear plan, it will give you the ability to reassess as you go along, seeing what is working as against what is not. You can then decide to change direction if need be to remain on the right track.

Watch out for the 'buying another job' syndrome
Remember the part you have agreed with yourself as to what you'll actually do in this business. Are you solely the captain of the ship navigating the way to your destination whilst the crew sail the boat for you, or are you a solo cross-Atlantic rower determined to get there under your own steam? Think about the different aspects, such as sourcing and project managing, lettings and management, accounts and admin—how much of this do you want to make passive on your part? It is advisable before you set sail on whichever journey you embark upon to know your own

strengths and passion and learn to let others support you in their designated roles. This may take time to fathom out and implement when you first start off, but rest assured, you'll get to know what you like and dislike and what you can delegate. If you find yourself regularly not enjoying the roles you have set out for yourself, you have fallen into the trap of just having bought yourself another job and that is the last place I want you to find yourself!

Knowing when to stop

So, you've been on your journey for a while now and one of three sets of circumstances will occur. You will either:

a) Reach your goal and celebrate! You will relish the fact that you have achieved what you set out to do and can now relax and enjoy the fruits of your labours or continue to build and grow your business to the next level.

b) Get to a certain point on your journey and question 'is this it...really?' You may decide that what you had expected has not been particularly forthcoming or enjoyable and decide that things either have to change or stop altogether.

c) You will feel like you are flogging a dead horse from the get go and at some point you will decide to stop.

Now, hopefully, if I have done what I have intended for this book, you will never face scenarios 'b' or 'c'! If I have not helped you to come to a decision about whether property is the right and best way for you to go, then either I haven't done my job properly or you have gone against your own gut feelings on the matter! I delight in helping people come to their own best conclusions through their decision to explore property as an option and take action as appropriate. The coaching and mentoring services I offer are tailor-made to each of my clients' requirements; I only work with people whom I *know* I can help. As a result, each person receives the individual attention they need, and in the vast majority of cases, end up with the results they seek. Again, a win/win scenario. To know more, visit www.whypropertyworks.co.uk/our-services/.

Knowing it will happen

I cannot emphasize this point enough—when you are certain about something, you are trusting the deepest part of yourself which knows best. When you know what you're doing and are wholeheartedly behind the decisions you make, then this really is the best space to invest from. Don't get me wrong, there will absolutely be an element of a 'leap of faith' on some deals you come across; it's just that inner knowing which will guide you along the way that you are looking for, to help you make decisions like that.

Mindset, belief and self-confidence

I know I have mentioned this more than a few times during this book, but it bears repeating; if you don't believe in yourself and what you are doing...who will?! As it all starts in the head, your head has to be in the right place in order for you to make the best decisions you possibly can.

Having a clear and positive mind helps you to focus on the task and actually go out from a position of strength. Imagine now knowing why you are investing, what your investment objectives are, what you need to look for in order to achieve this and how you're going to do it. How much more seriously will you be taken and how much more confident will you feel to go out and put it all together?

Another very important aspect of mindset is to have a 'can-do' attitude. You will very rarely go through a property transaction which runs totally smoothly, and if you can develop a solution-orientated way of thinking, anything that comes along to potentially trip you up, you will be able to deal with. Property investing is sometimes a rocky road, but with a positive mindset, you will see opportunities where others will see obstacles.

Intuition and gut feeling

Again, another topic I have covered but very important to reiterate at this point. I really had to learn to develop this during the course of my investing career. Every time I went against my better 'inner' judgement, the deal would come back to 'bite me on the bum'! I'm glad to say I learned very soon to heed these inner feelings and trust them rather than just my head, and I'm so glad I had these lessons early on. I have learnt that even when everything about the deal 'stacks up', you must listen to your gut feeling. I recommend that you do the 'sleep test' before agreeing to any deal you come across. If you are unable to sleep soundly and feel uncomfortable for some reason the night before you have to make that investment decision, then walk away. This also applies to when you have a 'too good to be true' feeling. It's your inner knowing and guidance which is subconsciously telling you the best course of action!

Trusting yourself and the process

When it comes to anything you do in life, you really *do* know what's best for you. Even during the times when you feel out of kilter or lacking direction, you will have moments of absolute clarity and will just *know* what to do instinctively. I think half the battle that most of us face is that we let our thoughts rule us most of the time, whereas if we let our innate instincts guide us, I'm sure we'd all be far better off!

If and when a 'problem' occurs during the course of your investment journey, you must learn to 'listen'. What on earth do I mean by this?! Well, it is in your reaction to and action taken during these types of events which define your character and your ability to handle your business. It is quite natural when you first start off to get emotionally involved and 'throw a wobbler' when something untoward happens and you end up reacting badly and potentially damaging your relationships with people. Watch out for this. If you can learn to take things on the chin and in most circumstances take responsibility for what has happened and then move on in a positive way, this will set you right for the longer term. If you find that things just 'keep happening' to you for 'no reason', dig deep and you will find that reason!

If it's really meant to be, it will predominantly flow easily. I remember how effortless it was for one of my clients to start investing because she was so relaxed about the process, had a clear and focussed mindset and knew exactly what she wanted to achieve (which was well within her scope of possibility) that a deal came to her within three days of us working together! I know you can say, 'right time, right place' and I'm sure there is an element of that, but I also believe that you have to be open to receive the types of opportunity that come along and you will attract the circumstance surrounding each of those deals. Hence why it is important to be clear and certain and feel chilled out about the whole process. Remember back to the rubber ring analogy...?!

Be practical

Being down-to-earth and just getting your head down in whichever way you choose to invest is by far better than carrying on contemplating it and talking but never doing. If you are clear about your investment objectives, just get going!

Are you sure you know what makes a good investment?
Before you go into any deal, you must take everything into account. Revising and practising the numbers is a must and something you need to become very good at, even if someone else is doing the donkey work for you! Remember, no one cares about your business as much as YOU! Calculate the TRR including your ROTI on each and every potential deal. It is now that you need to swat up again on the numbers as your business depends on this skill. Go back to Chapter 7 to do this if you can't remember! Only do the deal if everything is in alignment, the numbers stack up and it fits your investment requirements, otherwise, walk away...

Be proactive
Don't expect others to do things as quickly or efficiently as you would or might think they will. You must always remain proactive and on top of what is happening at each stage, otherwise you leave yourself open to delays and extra costs. You may sometimes feel as though you are doing everyone else's work; however, if it gets the job done then it is worth it. If you feel a sense of procrastination creeping in, nip it in the bud and just do whatever needs to be done. You'll feel much better and lighter rather than thinking you still have to do a particular task.

Keeping your word is a big one. When you say you'll do something, just do it! The number of times I have heard people say, 'I'll have the documents over to you by....' or 'I'll give you a ring next Monday about....' and it doesn't happen, to me is unprofessional and lazy. The simple answer is just don't promise what you can't deliver. If unforeseen circumstances occur and disrupt your schedule, which can and does happen, then of course that's understandable, but always aim to 'do what you say on the tin' as it were. It is important to keep in touch with people as much out of courtesy as keeping them informed.

Organisation and systems

I can't emphasize enough the importance of keeping records correctly and in order. At the end of the day, it makes life SO much easier, and you can delegate specific tasks much better if things are in a logical order. Keep all your research and due diligence records separate from the deals that actually go through—remember, property breeds paperwork! One top tip which I have still yet to master is 'never touch the same piece of paper (that includes post!) twice'. Hmmm....I wish! (Well, no one's perfect!) The principle is just to keep on top of things and know where everything is.

The ability to delegate aspects of your business is truly the key to you building a well-run, profitable and sustainable property business. If you get this factor right, you will be well on your way to achieving this.

The right formula

I'm sure if you spoke to 100 different investors you'd get 100 different answers as to the right approach to take and how to run your business, so this section really is just my take on what constitutes a winning formula. If you take a moment to think about how we achieve anything in life, we have to learn it first, put it into action next and review the outcome. It's simple really, so why don't we just follow the same formula for property investment and we'll head off in the right direction.

The right information and education

First and foremost in my mind is to seek out the right information from the right people. We all learn as we go along and continue to do so throughout our lives; however, a really good helping hand is invaluable in terms of adopting the right approach and knowing what things to consider as you embark upon or continue along on your own property journey. (Remember, just because someone else has done things in a particular way does not mean it is right for you. You must let your own intuition guide you, and so in terms of finding the right source of that external guidance, that is really down to you and who you feel would be the right person/company/course/etc./etc.) At the end of the day, there is a lot of great 'advice' out there. Just remember to keep to what 'sits right' with you when making your decisions.

If there is a particular method you have heard about and it appeals to you, then seek out the best person you can find to teach you how they've done it, and then if it does 'sit right', go for it. If, however, you are like most of the people I work with who either haven't really an idea of where to start or indeed which strategy would be best to work with, then you need someone who can navigate you through to making that decision and sort out what your best option is. When you do hit upon the strategy that feels best to you, then take guidance from the person or organisation who will best help to educate and inform you of the most useful processes and systems to utilise.

Again, beware the 'analysis paralysis' mode of operation which will stop you in your tracks. If you let your head get in the way too much, you may just miss the great opportunities and people out there who can help you. When making your choice, be certain that the person/organisation you are looking to work with knows and works within the remit of the law and understands the regulations (including building regulations and planning permission) and legislation involved—there are far too many people who don't. When all is said and done, you have to be able to sleep at night as it's your business you're dealing with.

The ability to make (the right!) decisions
You must be really wary of any decisions you make from either a greedy or a lazy place. You must be totally honest with yourself

when you are contemplating what the best course of action is on any particular project. If you discover there is a part of you which is just thinking, 'It's OK—it'll all work out for the best, I don't need to check this out any further', or 'Well, when this property values up to the highest value property in the street, I'm sure we'll get someone willing to pay full market value for it and it'll go really quickly. We don't really need to do 'X' or 'Y' on it and we can just cover over 'Z', so we can cut costs there, etc.', be warned! These thoughts will almost certainly end up with the boomerang effect!

Sometimes, the hardest decision is to choose *not* to do something. It takes a brave and courageous person to listen to their gut feeling, especially when your head is telling you 'everything's wonderful and rosy!' Again I repeat—if something just does not feel right about any part of your property activities, just walk away...

When, however, all things *do* stack up in the right way, then please, just do it!! I have seen a few people just stumble at this final point and fail to take action. This is what I mean when I say you have to recognise conducive circumstances yourself and *take action* on them. No one else will do this for you, and unless you have learnt how to recognise them, you will not see them. I hope this book has gone some way to you being now able to spot a good way forward when you see it!

It's a people business

If I've said it once, I've said it a thousand times—property is a people business, through and through. Learning these five great points about how to work with people will skyrocket you through:

1. Build rapport – without this you're dead in the water before you've even begun. If you're not naturally a 'people person', you may struggle with this. You can overcome

it with sheer practice and learning to become interested about people. If not, have someone else do it for you!

2. Be compassionate – no one will like you or want to work with you if you're hard-nosed and uncaring about someone's life situation. You will come across many types of characters in this business, and you have to be sympathetic to their lives when working with them, be they an agent, a vendor, a builder or a tenant.

3. Help others – if you can help as many people get what they want, you will ultimately get what you want... enough said!

4. Take responsibility – do not play the 'blame game' when something goes wrong. It will either have been out of someone else's control or if it is down to a particular person, learn from the lesson/mistake you made in working with them and choose a better person the next time! Getting angry and frustrated serves no one, least of all you.

5. Build a great team – this is not a one person game you are playing. Each of the people in your 'team' is crucial to your success. When building your team, ask yourself whether you have the best you can get and aim to develop long-term relationships with them. Be open, honest and transparent about your objectives, show respect and deal with any problems head on in a professional way. If any part of the team is not working, then get recommendations and look elsewhere to replace that person. When everything gels together, it is like a well-conducted orchestra (sorry, got carried away with my musical past there for a minute!!).

11. ENJOY the RIDE! PROPERTY INVESTMENT IS A ROLLER COASTER

Enjoy the ride!

Property investment is a rollercoaster journey of self-discovery!

WELL, WHAT CAN I SAY except that my property investment 'career' has been one of the scariest, most exciting, nail-biting and exhilarating rides of my life! It really has been a journey of ups and downs, slow uphill struggles and breathtaking moments of focus and 'full steam ahead'—I wouldn't have changed any of it for the world!

You learn so much about yourself

The minute you set foot on this path you will probably experience a number of emotions and reactions you probably never even knew you had in you. If you become aware of how you handle things as you go through, it'll teach you a great deal about yourself. If you're prepared to be really honest with yourself, you'll also see how your reactions and feelings about certain aspects 'show up' in other areas of your life. If you're willing to look and see these aspects of yourself, you will be led to a greater self-understanding and therefore to the best course of action for you to take.

How you handle problems or achievements will go a long way towards whether you succeed or fail in this business, and how quickly or slowly too. If you are willing to take a long, hard look at yourself when something doesn't go according to plan to see how you feel, you'll know soon enough whether you're on the right path, whether you may need to come back to it at another point or stop altogether.

Whatever happens, as you go along and learn your trade, you'll notice changes in yourself, how you become more tolerant, less emotional or stressed about the little things and even how you are more resilient and resourceful when the chips are down. All these changes in my experience (even and most of all through the toughest of patches) have been for the better.

The more you become self-aware, the better
As soon as you realise 'the buck stops here' in everything you do, the more empowered you become. You learn to make better decisions and become more efficient and effective in what you do—even in really small ways. Blaming others, as I've mentioned before, gets you nowhere very fast. When I think back to the experiences I described before in Chapter 6, it seemed that everything we were involved in with them was doomed! None of the investments worked out as we had anticipated, and at the time we literally felt sick to the stomach, angry at the directors of the company and furious towards the person who had introduced them to us. We found out during the course of time that they should have checked to see that we were high net worth individuals (which we weren't at the time) rather than pushing (that's how we felt anyway) us to 'hedge our investments' into other ventures which, when we've looked back since, were totally opposite to the objectives we were trying to achieve. When these investments didn't transpire as we'd hoped, we were the first to play the blame game and vented our anger and frustration at the company and the introducer. When we realised there

was almost nothing we could do except enter into a costly and time-consuming legal battle when we were already heading towards the iceberg like the Titanic, we knew there was only one thing for it...stop spiralling down the negative rabbit hole and get off our bums and do something about it. This was exactly what we did. We pulled out all the stops and were able to steer the ship back on course after a few months of sleepless nights, damned hard work and restructuring to make the portfolio stable again. We came out of it knowing that we really had no one else to blame but ourselves for having gone off course in the first place, taking someone else's advice against our own better judgement and being slightly lazy about the whole thing thinking the rewards would just drop into our laps like magic! We heard from them what we wanted to hear rather than heeding our own advice! A BIG lesson...

In the days when I was still a music teacher, I once heard the phrase 'the whole world is a mirror'. I contemplated this often, and when I stopped and became aware of it, I found it to be true. When you wake up in a foul mood or something 'puts' you in a bad mood, don't you just find your day turns out to be, well... pants?! Conversely, if you get out of the right side of the bed, things have a habit of just falling into place (mostly!). Watch and notice how people react to you during the course of a day. If you do this sincerely, you will notice that they really do reflect back the feeling you are 'putting out there'. Another way of saying this is 'perception is projection'. What you see in someone else is actually all about you! Crikey, when you take this on board—it *really* opens your eyes to how you are being! Equally, another useful thing to note when someone says something about you...it's actually about *them*! This is great for when the naysayers come along to tell you you're mad or that it's risky or could go wrong, etc., etc. They are seeing their own limitations in these opinions...as already mentioned, a useful tip to remember at times.

'What has this all got to do with property?!' I hear you cry! Well, if you can get a handle on these concepts, you will become a better investor. When I learned this 'stuff', I applied it to my investing and lo and behold, my success rate went up and the responses I had from people were much better. I have said all along that this has been more of a journey of self-discovery than property investing on many occasions! Having spoken and worked with many others along the way, I know it will be for you too.

Learn from every experience along the way

As you go along, check to see whether what you're doing actually works. Do a mini self-assessment on each aspect of your business if you're doing it yourself and ask yourself the hard questions like, 'Did that deal work?', 'Do I know my numbers well enough', 'Did I get out of this what I expected to?' and 'Am I still enjoying this?'

The world of property is a world of CPD (Continual Personal Development) just like any business or career these days. It is your responsibility to know and keep up-to-date with the laws and regulations. Joining a national body of landlords such as the National Landlords Association or the Residential Landlords Association will help you keep informed and on top of any new legislation coming in.

Take the time when building your portfolio to stop and take stock sometimes. Periods of consolidation can give you a valuable perspective on what you've achieved so far, what's gone well and not so well and whether you need to change strategy or reconfigure how you're doing things. It also gives you space to prepare for the next phase and ensure that everything is going according to plan.

Be yourself and do what you love!

It is really important that whatever decision you make in life, you are being true to yourself. If you make a decision and start to go along that route but then it starts to eat away at you, this is the time to reassess and decide differently if you are to really be true to yourself and do what makes you feel good.

The money will come from doing that which you enjoy and are good at

I meet and work with so many people who are dissatisfied with their work and/or work situation that it really made me grateful that I am passionate about (and good at!) what I do. Millions, probably billions of people go through their daily lives unsatisfied and unfulfilled (i.e., they haven't found their 'why'!) in one way or another. Most people put this down to 'human life' being as such, but there is a small minority which is starting to help wake people up to the fact that they don't have to remain in their status quo for the rest of their lives if they choose to do something about it. Let's face it, only a very small percentage of people actually enjoy the process of building a property business. The number of times I've had to pick people back up off the floor because they have given up their hated day job to become a full-time property investor, only to realise that it's not all a bed of roses and that the money doesn't necessarily come in thick and fast just because you have changed career!

My advice is if you really don't enjoy the work that you do or the life situation you're in and think property is the answer because it can bring in some good money...you're sorely mistaken. The best thing you could do is to stick at whatever you are doing and make a plan to move towards the direction of that which you *do* enjoy and are good at along the way until you can make the transition. I have helped many people to discover what it is they really want to be doing and then have created a plan so that property is used as a support mechanism around that. You can still (if you're in the right situation) put the money you make from your current occupation to work so that it builds up alongside what you're doing without you having to have much involvement, but you do have to totally trust the team of people who are doing this for you.

If you are fortunate enough to have a career you love and it's nothing to do with property, you can also apply this method to supplement your income as well as build vital funds for your pension pot. The vast majority of people I have worked with and continue to work with are those who know that property is a good idea and have a real interest in it, yet do not want it to take over their lives. You can quite easily 'buy yourself another job' if you're not careful, and it takes patience, care and planning to get a working model to help you achieve your goals without you being involved on a day-to-day basis. It is the reason I decided to 'go it alone' and set up my business, and the model I have devised works extremely well for people in this position. After all, you wouldn't choose to go and perform open-heart surgery on yourself, try to build your own vehicle or fly yourself to your holiday destination; you'd seek an expert in that field. Yet I see countless people going through seminar after seminar trying to do exactly this. So once and for all I am going to say *please*, stick to doing what is right for you and ask for help to do that which you can't or don't want to! Thank you! (Rant over!)

Doing this makes you more productive and gives you a 'zest for life'

I'm sure you know that feeling of 'being in the zone' and not knowing where the time went and not even feeling hungry when you're so into something. If you are able to spend more of your time in that place, then you will inevitably be more pro-ductive—you won't be able to help it! This in turn will produce better results and ideally more money so that you can then go ahead and get the help in where and when you need it on other projects.

Remember to reward yourself when you've done something which in your view was a real achievement. We rarely pat our-selves on the back and say 'you did good', so remembering to do so from time to time will spur you on and help you maintain that 'zest' for what you do. I am not talking about big rewards (unless you can and want to on certain projects), just a little acknowledgement to yourself by having an indulgent little treat which could be anything from a really good coffee and cake in your favourite cafe or taking an hour off to walk in the park or luxuriating in a nice warm bath when you wouldn't normally take the time.

You are not wrong if you don't do it all by yourself!
I used to be the world's worst for thinking I had to 'do it all'. As I've just said, getting people to help you perform certain tasks is not failure, in fact it's the most powerful thing you can do to leverage your time. How on earth would all the most successful business people on the planet do it if they didn't have the right people around them to help? The phrase 'no man is an island' is so true and so please know that there are people around to help you implement your dreams.

Learning to play to your strengths is a great way to begin the delegation process. Whether you intend to build and run your own portfolio or think about giving the task over to someone else, you must first remember to know what you are good at within the context and what you need to outsource. It may be that you're brilliant at working with people but weak on the numbers and organisation. This means you need someone to complement what you're not so good at so that you can work to your strengths and get the most benefit out of your time rather than struggling with and resenting the things you don't like doing.

If the thought of property investing (after having read through this whole book!) just makes you nervous, unhappy, stressed out, then don't do it! You're not wrong in making this discovery. You have just done yourself the best service by coming to that realisation before having spent much time, effort or money finding out that it's not a match. I commend you if you've been able to be this honest with yourself because it inevitably could have gone horribly wrong with those thoughts in mind. There are plenty of other things to invest your time, effort and money into in order to create wealth, and it's a question of sifting through the options to see which sits best with you. You can still apply much of what you have learned here on other forms of wealth creation to check whether they are right for you instead.

If, however, you're totally clear in knowing that property investment is right for you, then GREAT! Take the advice from this book and GET GOING! The next section will give you different options.

There are many different ways to invest – find the one which 'fits you best'

As there are so many different ways and strategies to adopt in terms of property investing, I will only deal with broad aspects here. It will be down to you to discover, either on your own or with help, the best course of action for you.

DIY investing

This is self-explanatory in that you will set-up, acquire and manage your own portfolio. It is the option for true lovers of all things property and business—even if you don't have the whole skill set to begin with but just have a knowing that this is the right choice for you. You might like to review Chapter 10 'What it really takes' to be certain this is the path for you.

Be prepared for long hours, patience, knowledge-gathering and lots of action in order to succeed. This is the route I went down, and as I have explained already, it is not for the faint-hearted! Don't get me wrong, the time and effort has truly paid off, and you earn amazing rewards if you do things this way, as long as you love it, enjoy it and are geared up to take the rough with the smooth sometimes along the way.

I work with a number of clients on this basis providing the guidance, expertise and experience I have gained over the many years I have been investing myself. Together, we can work through a complete programme which teaches you in-depth about all the key aspects needed to become a great investor. An important role I play is to help you take positive action and hold you accountable for what you need to do to get your business up and running. Depending on what stage you are at, I can help you to do a portfolio review or financial and strategic planning review right up to helping you on an ongoing basis for as long as you feel you need my support.

Totally 'hands off' armchair investing

I am personally very wary of this category. If you have no experience of investing, not only do you leave yourself open to the risks of not really knowing who you're working with (unless they have an exemplary and provable reputation), you also have really no clue of what you're investing in! The key is to really scrutinise who you're thinking of working with (see Chapter 6 'Cut the C**p' for guidance on this) as well as applying everything I've spoken about during the course of this book.

The negatives of investing this way are:

1. You don't know who you can trust
2. The potential risk factor of buying a deal 'blind'
3. Not knowing exactly what you're getting in terms of a 'deal'
4. High sourcing and management fees

The positives could be:

1. Very low time involvement
2. Less stress upfront
3. Good way to potentially build a 'hands off' pension pot

The companies which offer this type of service will always (of course) comment on the benefits of this type of scheme; however, there is a very real risk factor that you are putting your hard-earned cash into someone else's hands without really knowing much about the whys and wherefores. (Hmmm...sounds much like what happens in the context of pension funds these days...!) The most crucial factor apart from doing your due diligence and research up-front on the company/person is to then keep a really close eye on the ball.

The best of both worlds
To me, by far and away the best approach for the majority of people I meet and work with is to be able to work with a team

of people who can help you create what you are looking for. By doing this, not only do you massively leverage other peoples' time and experience but you also leverage your own time and resources by being able to continue with what you are good at and love doing or indeed need to be doing in order to set up your ideal lifestyle. By having someone 'do the leg work' for you (quite literally!), you have the freedom to spend as much or as little time on your investments as you can and want to. This approach is different to the hands-off 'armchair' approach in that you must also be aware, understand and be in control of what's going on in the portfolio-building process. Again, it is down to you to do your research to find the right person or people to be working with in terms of helping you achieve this, and I have already discussed this at length earlier in the book.

I actually believe in empowering people by teaching them exactly what they need to know in order to be efficient, effective and productive without having to spend their lives dedicated to it. I consider my coaching and mentoring style to be unique, and my main concern is to help people fulfil their 'why' through the processes I use. As far as I'm concerned, if I have taught somebody to *know* whether they are making a good investment decision and how to do it, then I have done my job properly! I take my role very seriously as I know it is peoples' lives, livelihoods, and financial futures I am dealing with. I am also of the opinion that people should be taking just as much of an interest in these things as me, rather than handing sole responsibility over to someone else to sort out for them.

I consider myself extremely fortunate to now be working with one of the best teams in the country. I met my business partner just as I started seriously thinking about setting up my own business and we clicked immediately. He shares the same passion for property, attention to client care and level of detail on his workmanship as I do. He is highly experienced (over 30 years in the industry) and works with only the best builders and trades people. We work together to help some of my clients in the way described above, and by using a truly sustainable model, we gear each person's requirements to create a 'best fit' solution for them. For more information on this or any other of my coaching and mentoring programmes, please contact me at www.whypropertyworks.co.uk.

The ultimate secret is to 'Be Happy Now'

Whether you think this sounds 'woo-woo', 'airy fairy' or 'hippy chick', the fact remains that unless you are truly enjoying your life, then you must ask yourself 'why am I doing it?'!!!

If you're not, what's the point?

I don't believe we're meant to go through this life to suffer unnecessarily, and if we have a choice about what we do with it (which we all do!) then surely you'd choose the things which make you happy—wouldn't you?! You can have all the goals and dreams in the world and think, 'When I have £X amount in the bank, then I'll be happy' or 'When I am sitting behind the wheel of that Ferrari I've always dreamed of, then I'll be happy' or 'When I am financially free, can sack my boss and relax on a beach for the rest of my life, then I'll be happy' (and so the story goes on...). Well, I'm here to tell you that's BULLS**T!!! Those things *won't* make you happy. It's the process by which you attain these things which will ultimately make you or break you, and wouldn't you rather do it joyfully than miserably slogging away? If you were to carry on like that, then even when you have those things, it won't make a difference because you'll create yourself a whole new set of problems. My message is don't wait until you have achieved your property goals to be happy—they won't. If you're not happy building it, you won't enjoy owning and running it either.

Make a list of what makes you happy

When was the last time you sat down and really considered what makes you happy? Chances are you never have! So here's your opportunity now to grab a pen and scribble away...

EXERCISE

10 things which make me happy

E.g., Watching my children laugh, going out for a really good meal with friends, taking the time to walk in the park and breathe fresh air, seeing the sun set with my favourite wine in hand, etc., etc.

1. _____
2. _____
3. _____
4. _____
5. _____
6. _____
7. _____
8. _____
9. _____
10. _____

Did you do it? I hope so—it's quite an addictive exercise when you let you mind wander. When I suggest this to clients and they actually implement it in their lives, I can see the transformation take place in front of me over time. I see and feel a sense of ease come back into play rather than stress and angst. The more they do this, the more joy, peace and life satisfaction they report back to me. Admittedly, you do have to be open to the idea of doing this, and for some it feels strange—but that's only because the concept of truly enjoying life on a regular basis has been sucked out over years of conforming and giving in to the idea that life has to be hard. Take and make the time to do things that make you happy more often and notice how you feel when you do. The more you practise it and become aware of it, the more enjoyment you'll get out of life.

If you don't, you could literally waste years of your life. This may sound hard, but I've worked with so many people, who are to certain degrees unhappy with their lot, that the shift has to be made on the inner level before it can be truly demonstrated on the outside, in their life. Ask yourself the question, 'What am I doing all this for anyway?' I can assure you that if you really do take this on board, then you will not want to be dependent on some future event to make you happy; the idea is to be happy NOW.

The more you do this, the more circumstances you'll bring into your life which will make you even happier, and you'll have a sense of lightness about you rather than the 'weight of the world'. This is where the law of attraction comes into play and reflects back to you that which you are 'putting out there'.

If this all sounds very philosophical, that's because it's meant to! I can say from both personal experience and the experiences of those I have had the pleasure of working with that this really does work and count towards that which you are trying to achieve the most. If you discover this 'secret' for yourself, you'll build your portfolio easily, effortlessly, sustainably and profitably for many years to come. Take note of which parts of this book resonate with you most as they will be your own best personal guide for your journey ahead.

Why Property Works

Unlocks The Secrets of Successful Property Investment

1. PROPERTY

and YOU

→ How to know if property investment is right for you ←

YOU

2. THE IMPORTANCE of KNOWING YOUR 'WHY'

→ Your driving force ←

3. It's **NOT** about the **MONEY**!

LOVE

4. Start with the RIGHT investment

MINDSET

→ It's all in your head ←

GOAL!

OBST. ACLE

5.

How to deal with what's STOPPING you

In Conclusion

So, we come to the end of our journey together...or perhaps not! Perhaps it's just the beginning... Having read through this book, you will have gained insights into the world of property which you may not have come across before. Now it's time to make a decision. Which way will you go? For starters, you may like to continue to join me on your property quest by going to the Next Steps page overleaf. As I have already mentioned, I work with people on a regular basis through my property mentoring and coaching programmes. I find that the work we do together acts as a significant springboard to success. I love what I do...seeing people achieve results they only imagined possible actually happening is incredibly rewarding. Knowing that I am helping someone secure their financial future through sound methodology and good practice is an incredible place to be and for that I am truly grateful. If you would like to be a part of what we do, how we do things and most importantly why we do things then feel free to contact us.

Whatever your decision from here on, I wish you every success and happiness in your property journey and would like to thank you again for taking the time to read my thoughts on this subject. It is my heartfelt gratitude towards each and every part of my own journey that has enabled me to put these words down on paper and hopefully make a difference to you. Thank you.

Next Steps

If you haven't already, remember to check out the extra gifts and training materials I have put together just to help you get started...

Have fun!

Golden Rules for Successful Property Investment |
An Investor's Essential Guide

Property Business Tools | Designed to help you gain good insights into certain aspects of running your property business

Online Training Videos | Enjoy the expertise from the comfort of your own home and learn at a pace which suits you

Live Events | Check to see where Hazel
is speaking in the coming months

Communities | Join like-minded investors

Testimonials | Check out the testimonials from our clients

Bespoke Mentoring and Coaching Programmes | Take your investing to the next level and start creating or developing your own cash-flowing portfolio | Our specialist services are tailored to match your needs exactly in terms of property acquisition and management

For Instant Access, visit:
www.whypropertyworks.co.uk/get-started/

Glossary of terms

PCM – Per Calendar Month

JV – Joint Venture

HMO – House of Multiple Occupation

BTL – Buy-to-Let

DLR – Docklands Light Railway

LTV – Loan to Value

DIY – Do it Yourself

LTD – Limited Company

P.A. – Per Annum

ROI – Return on Investment

ROTI – Return on Time Invested

YIELD – The gross rental return on a property

TRR – True Rate of Return

GSC – Gas Safety Certificate

ESC – Electrical Safety Certificate

PAT tests – Portable Appliance Testing

FSC – Fire Safety Certificate

EPC – Energy Performance Certificate

AST – Assured Shorthold Tenancy

DPS – Deposit Protection Service

TDS – Tenancy Deposit Scheme

NLA – National Landlords Association

RLA – Residential Landlords Association

FREEHOLD – The ownership of real property

LEASEHOLD – Property which reverts to the owner once the lease has expired

TITLE DEEDS – Documents showing ownership, rights, obligations or mortgages on a property

LAND REGISTRY – The national system of land registration

BUILDING CONTROL – A set of rules that specify minimum standards for the construction of buildings

PLANNING PERMISSION – The permission required to be allowed to build on land or change the use of land or buildings

CPD – Continued Personal Development

About the author

Hazel de Kloe is the founder and Head Mentor of Why Property Works, which mentors and coaches people from a variety of backgrounds and levels of property experience. Helping people to maximise their potential within the property industry, Hazel is recognised as one of the UK's leading Property Mentors. Having been a finalist at the National Landlord Association Property Women Awards and Kent Women In Business Awards within the first year of business, she also regularly writes articles for the UK's largest franchised property business, Martin & Co. Hazel is regularly asked to speak at various property networking and business events around the UK and also contributes to helping young people understand the importance of creating sound financial foundations.

Book reviews

"This book is a must read for anyone thinking about property investing. Hazel's advice and guidance will help you decide if property investment is the right decision for you. Reading her book felt like I was in one of her coaching sessions with her high energy and passion but grounded no-non-sense approach."
CHERYL WILTSHIRE

"What I found really refreshing about Hazel's book is that she tells the reader the truth. Most books on the subject hype property investment up making out its easy and that everyone should do it. If this was the case why aren't we all millionaires? Hazel's book gives an honest and concise insight into property investment. She gives sound advice and tangible case studies. 'Why Property Works' is an absolute must read for anyone venturing out into the unpredictable world of property investment.

Hazel is a remarkable and inspirational woman. She's extremely knowledgeable about the property world due to her extensive experience, she's hardworking, creative in her thinking, professional, and reliable. Not only that but Hazel is a thoroughly decent and down to earth person. She cares more than the usual person and genuinely wants to help for all the right reasons. She has a lovely humour and positivity about her. She has a great perspective and balance on life which is lovely to be around. She has made this 'journey' possible for me and in such an enjoyable, relaxed, confident way. I can't recommend working with Hazel enough."
SARAH MAN

"Hazel de Kloe's excellent first book will help you to change your life through property investing. Whatever your dreams, whether they be fi-nancial freedom, escape from the rat race, or finding a way to earn a

living while exploring remote tropical islands, this book will help you to achieve them. 'Why Property Works' contains everything you need to find your "Property Why", the motivating force which will power you towards success, as well as many of the secret techniques used by the professionals to create wealth through property investment."
WILL PAICE

"We came to Hazel at a time when we had already been severely bitten by quite a few of the property sharks out there...

To be honest, I wish we had come across her book way before we had ever embarked on the property buying journey. Her book is without a doubt, an absolutely definitive guide to getting into the property market. If you have never done it - buy the book! If you ate just starting out and con- sider yourself to still be a novice - you will certainly find the book useful.

Hazel de Kloe succinctly covers all angles. She takes you through the motions, guides you, hold your hand if you needs it. Hazel is skilled at pointing you in the right direction. She can only advise you of what to do & where to go. The rest is ultimately up to you.

It is a journey, one that needs to be learned to enjoyed. Yes, do your due diligence. Be ruthless. Be bold. But, be sensible. This is where Hazel excels! She has experienced a lot - so learn from her!"
AMANDA THOMAS & ANNETTE STEIN

"Having known Hazel personally from using her mentorship services I was intrigued to read this book. All I can say is I wish I had met Hazel 5 years ago.

In an industry full of snake oil salesman Hazel is one of only a hand- ful of people I have met in the Property Education world that has true integrity and really tells it like it is. Forget the expensive seminars and smooth talkers telling you how to build a portfolio with methods that are not even legal anymore.

If you want to find out what is really involved, understand there is no magic bullet and that hard work will be required then please read this book first!

You won't regret it."
JAY WRIGHT

"Hazel's book for me really challenges the thinking about property and makes you think about why you are doing it which is so important as it's not just about the money! I love the analogies she uses and her slow approach which leads to sustainability. I have chosen to work with Hazel as I believe she genuinely wants to help me on my journey."
JULIE GEDDES

"Having worked with Hazel a little before reading her book, I can honestly say that her personality comes through onto the page. I can recommend this book, especially to those thinking about starting on the road to Property Investment. I found it useful as a novice in "getting my head round" the whole subject. Hazel's approach, of understanding why you want to invest in property, helps you focus better on the whether this is indeed the right path for you. Honest, straightforward facts and good advice, with no hype. Plenty of common sense, not exaggerated promises of instant wealth. All in easy to understand plain English: even the calculations are carefully explained and easily understandable. A very readable book."
IMOGEN EAST

Speaking testimonials...

I have known Hazel for over five years and during that time I have been touched by her generosity as a human being and her compassion towards others. As an international speaker I meet many people, some you have a greater impact on me than others, Hazel is one of the rare people who will stick in your heart. She has a great gift for teaching and inspiring others whilst making her message relatable and genuine. Her success in business and life and in recent years as a Mentor makes her a great messenger for success and abundance. To have Hazel as a guest speaker at my events is always an honour. Enjoy your time with her...

DR ROHAN WEERASINGHE,
ENTREPRENEUR AND PROFESSIONAL SPEAKER

Hazel De Kloe recently presented "Why Property Works " at Harlow Property Network Meeting. Hazel presented a thought provoking presentation, challenging our members to question their reasons for investing in property and determine what they really want to achieve through property. Both experienced and new investors will gain invaluable knowledge from listening to Hazel.

FRANCES LONG, HARLOW PROPERTY NETWORK

I have no hesitation in inviting Hazel back to Wandsworth Property Networking. Hazel has already attended Wandsworth Property Network as a panel member and speaker. If you are thinking of inviting Hazel to your networking event - don't think twice - book here before her diary becomes full. She is an amazing presenter and I don't always say this.

BRENDAN QUINN,
WANDSWORTH PROPERTY NETWORK

Whatever your strategy is in property it is ultimately about people, making a good impression and creating good long term relationships – when I first met Hazel a few years ago at a property networking event her integrity and honesty shone through; she was professional and very easy to talk to.

With over 12 years property experience Hazel can share real nuggets of the Do's and Don'ts of building a portfolio and can inspire and help both new and experienced investors.

"What does it take to be a successful Property Investor" – besides mindset, belief and self confidence its knowing your "Why" – Hazel will practically explain the process with the audience which received great feedback at our event in November.

After the meeting our attendees used words to describe Hazel's presentation such as "Passionate", "Inspiring" and "Easily approachable".

MARTIN BURT – PROPERTY INVESTOR, TRADER
AND CO HOST OF THE KENT PROPERTY CLUB

Clients say...

We worked closely with Hazel as part of a mentoring program and can truthfully say that she was a great source of knowledge and enthusiasm. Hazel's guidance helped us to see the bigger picture and gave us the confidence and tools to push our property business forward to new heights. Since working with Hazel we have done a number of property deals and are currently working on a 2 flat conversion nearby. Our property portfolio is now looking healthy and the future is looking great. I would say to anyone getting started or even in this business already that "knowledge is king but choose the source of that knowledge wisely". We did and can only offer our heartfelt thanks for Hazel's help.
STEVE AND KAY BENNALLACK – CORNWALL

I found Hazel very focused. She worked with great clarity and was able to separate what appeared to be important and what is important. She uses a holistic approach as a business mentor which I felt is the only way forward, looking at what motivates you, blocks you and moves you on. The most useful part of working with Hazel was looking at the emotional rationale behind why you are in business. Focusing on the passion within yourself and highlighting how to make that work for you as opposed to running after money for the sake of it! It's a totally different way at looking at business; there is a plan to what Hazel does – it's thorough and organised.
CATHI HARGADEN – WINDSOR

Hazel is a perfect mentor and coach; sincere, very helpful, understanding, patient, experienced and friendly – an excellent mentor and coach. What I found most useful was that she found solutions for the problems that I had, sorting out real problems that I had, but not lecturing something general. The result of working with her has been that I've found a sourcing agent, an accountant, a broker and have got a mortgage in principle in place. It is a pleasure to learn and work with Hazel, because she is such a natural, honest and decent person with a lovely sense of humour.
ALEX MARKOV – LONDON

Hazel has great integrity and business acumen and can work on the big picture as well as process flows – which is a rare combination! One of the most important points to me was that I always felt that she cared as much about the person as she did about the results. She really tried to understand what motivated me and would continue to do so in the long run. Hazel's common sense approach demystified the whole property world for me. She made it easier (not easy!) and fun and broke down all processes into bite-sized chunks. I am very good at amassing theory, she made me apply it! Working with Hazel is a pleasure as she brings so much energy to the table that you can't help but feel empowered.

KARIN HUETTL – MILTON KEYNES

At the time, I was already an experienced investor, on the verge of retiring from the 'day job' and merely spending a couple of days per week developing our portfolio to increase its size and income. Jan and I both enjoyed working with Hazel and found that we worked well together. We found Hazel very knowledgeable on the subject of property. She brought a professional and 'business like' approach to the mentorship and addressed 'mind-set' and negotiation skills which we found to be a very important aspect. We achieved our objective for the time we spent together securing a freehold block of 3 flats at 20% BMV when 'all monies in', including refurbishment and the costs of purchase were taken into account as well as a yield of £375 pcm net. Hazel knew people who had used the strategy in our selected area and prior to working with us, she obtained contacts for us to meet. We have continued to invest in property and widen the range of strategies that we use.

PETER AND JAN NICHOLSON – ESSEX

Hazel has been an inspiration to us and we would recommend you a spare an hour of your time to potentially make real changes to your life. We found our sessions exciting, fun and we always felt uplifting during and after our sessions. Hazel cares about her clients and it shows in her listening and questioning. She helped us to see our life more clearly, how to be more proactive in our life and how to achieve our goals. Her passion is working with people to realise their dreams, she is so

positive, down to earth, very kind, friendly and warm person. We are truly grateful to her.
KRISTINA AND MIRO CHRAPKA

Having thought I had what it took to become a property investor, I still felt I needed that extra confidence boost and experience a Property Mentor would bring to allow me, to take the next steps.

I found Hazel by chance, online, through her web site "Why Property Works" and after watching her promotional video, my "gut instinct" was to take the next step and book an initial consultation to meet with Hazel. I am pleased to say my trusty "gut instinct" was spot on, Hazel was just the kind of Mentor I was looking for, professional, friendly, experienced and knowledgeable, just want I was going to need to get me started.

Hazel has now been my coach and mentor for 5 months, she has always been there to answer any questions I have, listening to my ideas and steering me in the right direction. In the past I have been very risk adverse and this has been the biggest hurdle for me to overcome. With Hazel's help I now fully understand my "Why" and just as important my "How" in growing a successful property portfolio. This knowledge has significantly reduced my fear of the risks involved and I am now looking forward to achieve the goals we have set for the next 18 – 24 months.
TINA LOCOCK

My name is Marisa and together with my boyfriend we have been researching and "studying" about property investment at least for the last 6 months. Once we decided that we wanted to know more and be serious about it, we signed up for a coaching programme from a company based in the States where we had 30 mins sessions every week for 2 months. However this was a great start and we learnt a whole philosophy, the coach was never available to review our homework, the customer service line was always busy and having a coach that wasn't an expert in the UK market really has held us back from making a decision about our first purchase.

I met Hazel through a friend that I did in the mentioned course. As soon as I contacted Hazel, she replied straight away and was very accommodating to have our initial free 30 minute conversation over Skype. We ran through our whole story and we decided that it would really help us make a decision to have a 3 hour session.

I don't have words or can't explain how much value, knowledge, experience and sense Hazel brought to our game. Hazel came to the session well prepared with articles and meaningful reading for us, she had her own structure but first of all, we've reviewed all our questions and concerns together, this way she ensured that she used our time wisely to cover everything. Hazel asked many questions, read through all our preparation, analysed our options (even with the calculator) and guided us through the best way going forward for us. Before the session, we were still very unclear about our decision but after the session we were clear and secure about it. She helped us so much that I can't even describe it. I also felt that Hazel shared all her knowledge with us, from the small details (how much changing a carpet would cost) to the bigger picture and 5-10 year scenario. I strongly and genuinely recommend Hazel, she has given us the confidence and the boost we needed and she will definitely will be our guide in this very first step. Thanks a million Hazel.

MARISA ZAPPATORE

Lightning Source UK Ltd.
Milton Keynes UK
UKOW06f1152300815

257734UK00002B/42/P

Die Vogel : Ein Lyrisch-phantastisches Spiel In Zwei Aufzügen : Op. 30

Braunfels, Walter, 1882-1954, Aristophanes. Birds

WALTER BRAUNFELS

DIE VÖGEL

KLAVIERAUSZUG MIT TEXT

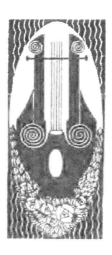

UNIVERSAL-EDITION

DIE VÖGEL

Ein lyrisch - phantastisches Spiel in zwei Aufzügen
nach Aristophanes

Dichtung und Musik von

WALTER BRAUNFELS

Op. 30

Klavierauszug mit Text

Aufführungsrecht vorbehalten. Droits d'exécution réservés

UNIVERSAL-EDITION A. G.

WIEN Copyright 1920 by Universal-Edition LEIPZIG

VORBEMERKUNG

Man wird bemerken, daß ich nur im ersten Akt der Aristophanischen Vorlage einigermaßen gefolgt bin Unter den von mir zu Rat gezogenen Übertragungen des Urtextes verdanke ich am meisten der von Dr Schinck (Reclam, Leipzig) Für einzelne Wendungen, besonders des Wiedhopfes – Seite 44 und 55 – und des Ratefreund – Seite 82 – 86 – fand ich in der Nachdichtung von Dr Owlgass (bei Diederichs) glückliche Vorlage In Hoffeguts romantischem Gesang in der Nachtszene des zweiten Aktes (Seite 117 – 118) konnte ich es mir nicht versagen, Eichendorffsche Verse einzuflechten

WALTER BRAUNFELS

PERSONEN:

Stimme des Zeus . . . . *Bariton*	1 Meise . . . } *Sopran*
Prometheus . . . *Bariton*	2 Meise . .
Wiedhopf, einstens ein Mensch, nun	1 Wendehals . .
König der Vögel . . *Bariton*	2. Wendehals . . . . } *Tenor*
Nachtigall . . *Hoher Sopran*	3 Wendehals .
Zaunschlüpfer . *Sopran*	4 Wendehals
1 Drossel . . . . *Tiefer Sopran*	1 Kibitz . . } *Baß*
2 Drossel .	2 Kibitz . . .
1 Schwalbe	Adler . *Baß*
2 Schwalbe . *Sopran*	Rabe . . *Baß*
3 Schwalbe	Flamingo . . . *Tenor*

Tauben, Grasmücken, Kuckucke, Spechte, Ibisse, Kraniche, Störche Enten und andere Vögel

Hoffegut } Bürger einer großen Stadt { . . . *Tenor*
Ratefreund }	. . *Hoher Baß*

Stimmen der Winde und der Blumendufte

PERSONEN DER TANZSZENE
Taube und Taubrich

UNIVERSAL-EDITION AKTIENGESELLSCHAFT
WIEN   LEIPZIG

Die Vögel.

Vorspiel und Prolog.

Walter Braunfels, Op. 30.

Langsam und zart.

Klavier.

Copyright 1920 by ... Universal-Edition Nr. 6420, 6428.

Der Vorhang wird nur ein wenig zur Seite gezogen; man gewahrt die Nachtigall, auf einem buschigen Baume sitzend.
Scheinbar überrascht mustert sie das Publikum, dann beginnt sie kühl und kokett.

Lieb - - wer - te Freun - de, ge-

grüßt, heut weilt ihr in uns'rem Rei - - che, wo das

Le - ben leicht den Fro - hen fließt, je - de Stun - de neu - e Freu-de ge-

biert; von vol - lem Herz spricht sü - ßer

ERSTER AUFZUG.

Felsige Berggegend mit viel Gebüsch und wenigen Bäumen zur Mittagszeit. Hoffegut und Dickle, Ratefreund eine Krähe auf der Hand tragend, kommen mühsam über die Felsen geklettert. Sie haben Zwerchsäcke umgeschnallt, aus denen allerlei Kochgerät herausschaut.

Wie konnt' er sa - gen, die - se zwei - ge - fie - der - ten Ka - na - il - len

sie wer - den uns sich - ren Wegs zum Wied-hopf füh - ren,

der den Vö - geln Kö - nig ist!

(Die Dohle pickt auf ihn ein.)

Al - lein die Bles-ter bei - ßen nur. Du schnappst schon wie-der? Willst du uns denn den

13

(Sie suchen

Fels hin - un - ter schmeißen? Nir - gend ist ja ein Weg!

vergeblich zwischen den Felsen nach dem Weg)

Ratefreund.

Auch nir-gends nicht die Spur

Hoffegut.

Da sit - zen wir nun fest!

... von ei-nem Weg!

Ra - ben-fraß!

14 Ratefreund.

Und war der Zweck doch so be-son - ders, der von den Men-schen

weg mich trieb: nicht an schön kommt' Ich, wie auf Er - den die Kunst,

die hol - de, hol - de Kunst ent - ar - tet.

Ich sehn-te mich nach Vög-leins si-ben Tri - ri - li

Lebhafter.

Ratefreund.

Ha, sieht so das Stück-chen Er-de aus, das frei von Chi-ka — nen

Lebhaft.

Hoffegut.

He____ du!

ist.

Was giebt es?

Lebhaft.

Klar.

Hoffegut.

Herr — lich, mei-ne Doh — le sperrt den Schna — bel auf,

ge-wiß, du dro — ben will sie uns was zei-gen, Ich möch-te

U. E. 3420.

20

C. 1. 16420.

(er klopft mit einem Stein auf einen aus dem Buschwerk herausragenden Felsen)
Hoffegut.
Hop-hop, hop-hop! Hop-hop, hop-
R.
ru-fen, „Bursch“ ver-steht er nicht.
sf
f
H.
hop! Hop,hop, hop,hop, hop,hop, hop hop, hop,hop,hop,hop,hop,
H.
hop, hop, hop, hop, hop, hop... ha-ha-ha-ha-ha-ha-ha!
f
senza dimin.
22
Zaunschlüpfer (hinter der Szene).
Wer ist denn da? Ruft je-mand hier nach mei-nem
p
pp
Hr. ged.
pp

(Hier betritt **Zaunschlüpfer** die Bühne. Auf's höchste erschreckt, weichen
Hoffegut und Ratefreund bis zum Rande des Proscenlums zurück.
Dohle und Krähe fliegen davon.)

*) Auf dieses Achtel sollen die Konsonanten get accentuiert gesprochen werden.

U. E. 6426.

24

29

Allmählich etwas fliessender.

Ta - - ten wie noch seit Welt - bestehn sie kein Ge-schlecht gesehn, so

ü - ber-mäss' - gen, so ge-walt - gen, nie ge - tung' - nen, nie be - sung' - nen,

nie ge - träum-ten Ta - - ten ist der Vö-gel Volk be-

Wiedhopf.

Was sol-len wir denn tun?

stimmt Er - baut euch ei - ne

Wol - ken bau - et ei - ne Burg, die kühn - sten Stür - men

fp

l.H.

fp

Wiedhopf.

Wie - so denn?

bie - tet Trotz, aus - hun - gern könnt ihr die Göt - ter dann!

mf

f

50

Ist zwi - schen Erd' und Him - mel nicht die Luft?

p

l.H.

Ihr sperrt sie ab mit un - ge - beu - rem Krei - se.

p

12/8

51

Und wenn nun die Menschen den Himm-li-schen op-fern und euch nicht er-le-gen ge-büh-ren-de

Zöl-le, ge-wührt ihr der Op-fer er-quik-ken-den Dün-sten fort-an kei-nen Durchzug mehr durch eu-re

To-re, und al-so-bald geht ihr den Göt-tern zu Lei-be, die heu-te so si-cher da dro-ben sich

wöh-nen, doch weil sie der dampfen-den At-zung be-dür-fen, gar bald eu-re Gna-de er-flehn:

cresc.

50

hop po-po-po-po-po-po pop, ti-o. ti-o. o-he! Ihr all, die ihr in

Gär-ten na-schet, d' ihr auf Ber-gen Bee-ren pik-ket.

Ah,_____ ah._____ Ah!

Ti-o._____ ti-o, ti-o, ti-o,

63

Hop po-po-po-po-po-po-po-po pop   o-he!   Die auf tau-i - - gen

espress.

Nachtigall.

Ah.

Wie - - sen fröh - lich ihr wei - det, her -

Ah.

bei!

espress.

cresc.

mf

(Von allen Seiten beginnen nun die Vögel unter großem Lärmen zusammen zu strömen; erst einzelne wie z. B. Schwalben, dann im bunten Wechsel immer zahlreichere.)

60

64

(Storch schreitet gravitätisch, im Rhythmus mit dem Schnabel klappernd, um die beiden Menschen herum.)

Hoffegut.

Sieh' nur die - se Vo - gel-scha - ren, wie sie trip-peln, wie sie pie - pen, zet - tern, krächzen, um uns flat - tern

mit Ge-kreisch!   O je, o je, das Vo - gel-zeug, o

Ratefreund.

We - - he, weh, mit off - nem Schna - bel kom - men al - le auf uns zu!

Wiedhopf.

Schwal - be, Hä - her, Hüh - ner-vo - gel, Mei - se, Ki - bitz, Specht und Tau - be,

je, o je, das Dros - sel-zeug.

(schreiend)

Sie be - dro-hen uns zwei bei-de!

Bruch - weiß-kehl - chen, Rot - hals-tau - cher, Krä - he, Kra - nich, Falk' und Storch!

66

71

G. E. 6120.

80 Etwas mäßiger.
Wiedhopf.

Kam einst nicht Ich zu euch als Freund, lehrt' euch die

Spra - che, man - cher-lei Sit - ten, wünschtet selbst, daß Ich bei euch

blieb; War es so? War es so?

Kam so von Menschen je euch Freundschaft. so sind Freun - de die - se

auf _____ der Er - de schür - fen sie Schät - ze, glit - - zern-de Stei - ne,

auf der Er - de gibt es

auf der Er - de _____ gibt es

bun - te Per - len, ja _____

Schät - ze, si - cher bringen sie uns hel - le Per - len,

Schät - ze, _____ si - cher bringen sie uns hel - le Per - len,

Chor der Vögel.

Sopr. *pp*

Er soll re - den,

Alt. *pp*

Er soll re - den,

84

p

Ratefreund.

Wie tut ihr Vög-lein nur leid, daß ihr nicht mehr Kö - ni - ge seid.

Sopr. *p*
Kö - ni - ge, wir,

Alt. *p*
Kö - ni - ge, wir,

Ten. *p*
Kö - ni - ge, wir,

Baß. *p*
Kö - ni - ge, wir

R.
Ü-ber al - les, was lebt, ü-ber mich, ü-ber den; ja, selbst,

Herrn, ü - ber wen?

Herrn, ü - ber wen?

Herrn, ü - ber wen?

Herrn, ü - ber wen?

mf

R. Kein Mensch bei den Göt - tern einst schwur, nein, bei den Vö - geln

äl-ter sind wir als Kro - nos.

äl-ter sind wir als Kro - nos.

äl - ter wie Kro - nos.

äl - ter wie Kro - nos.

R. schwu - ren sie al - le; so ha - ben sie in frü - he - rer Zeit al - le euch

R. hoch_ und hei - lig ge - hal - ten, sie euch hoch ge - hal - ten.

(Die Vögel blicken einander mit seliger Gebärde an.)

Ratefreund.

Und wie ist es jetzt?

Wie

wü - ten - de Hun - de wirft man euch tot, man fängt euch in Schlin - gen, in Netz und Garn, ein

fordert ihr kühn von Zeus die Herrschaft zurückzugeben; du zu sich nicht

gleich bereit, so erklärt ihr mutig ihm den Krieg.

93 (Freudige Bewegtheit der Vögel)

Auch die Menschen sollen opfern euch.

sonst trifft sie euer grimmer Zorn gleich einem

Fast doppelt so langsam.

95 **Hoffegut.** (In zarter Ergriffenheit, mit erhobenen Armen.)

Ach, der Zeit, wir zie-hen fort-an nicht zum Op-fer nach Del-phi

mehr; wir tre-ten fort-an zum Fei - gen-baum, streu'n ver-

ch - rend sü - ße Kräu - ter euch, flo - hen euch mit er - hob - nen

Hän - den an, o be-schee - ret uns vom Gu - ten ein Teil!

Das wird uns dann auch ge - währt, ja

und Se - - - - nen - blü - te

strö - met auf uns, ü - ber al - le Ir - di - schen aus!

Fast

Wiedhopf.

Nun

97 doppelt so schnell.

ist nicht Zeit zum Zau - - - - - - dern mehr, tut

von euch al - le Säu - mig - keit, macht euch be - reit mit Em - sig - keit zum

gro - ßen Werk: Aus Ly - bi - en ver - sam - melt mir zehn - tau - send Kro - at -

(Die bezeichneten Vögel fliegen sogleich fort.)

98

N.
Fül — — — le ü — ber uns strö — men, uns all — er — schau — en — de,

2.
Tag schenkt uns Glük — kes Fül — — le, uns all — er — schau — en — de,

Dr.
se — — lig ü — ber uns strö — men, uns all — er — schau — en — de,

N.
all — er — freu — en — de, all ge — lieb — te All — be — herr — scher!

L.
all — er — freu — en — de, all ge — lieb — te All — be — herr — scher!

Dr.
all — er — freu — en — de, all ge — lieb — te All — be — herr — scher!

Hoffegut.
Die

Wiedhopf.
Die

Sopran.
Al — le

Alt.
Al — le

Tenor.
Die

Baß.
Die

CHOR.

poco a poco cresc.

Lebhaft.

(Alle Vögeln flattern, wie aufgescheucht, empor und sind im Augenblick verschwunden.)

Pla - ge birgt.

Pla - ge birgt.

Pla - ge birgt.

Pla - ge uns birgt.

Pla - ge uns birgt.

Pla - ge birgt.

Pla - ge birgt.

Pla - ge uns birgt.

Pla - ge uns birgt.

Lebhaft.

dimin.

(Rotefreund der stolz gebläht seinen Schmuck zu betrachten sucht, scheint nichts zu bemerken. Hoffegut blickt den Vögeln nach.)

ZWEITER AUFZUG.

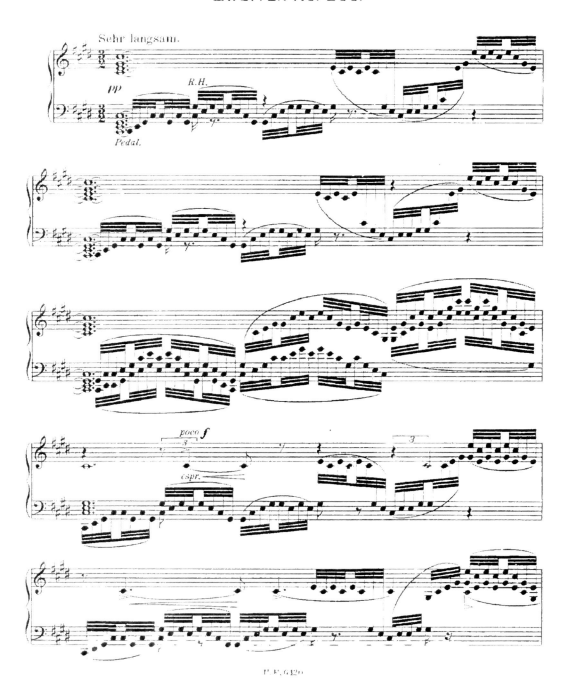

108

Etwas gedehnt.

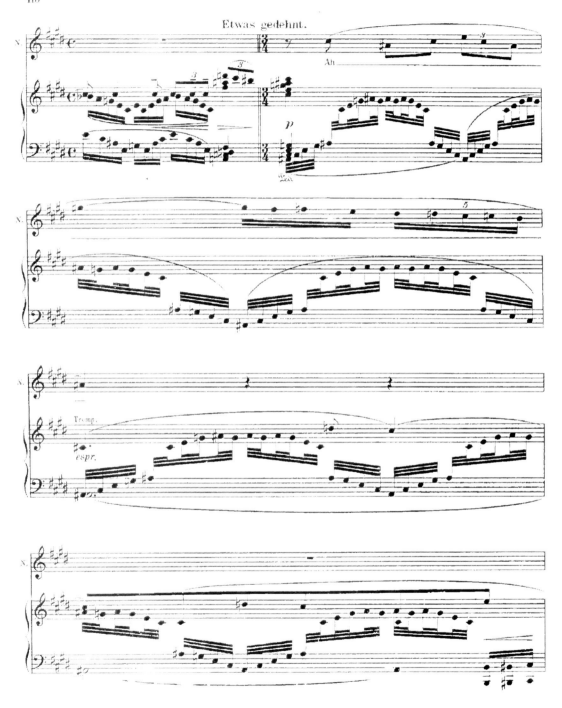

Ah

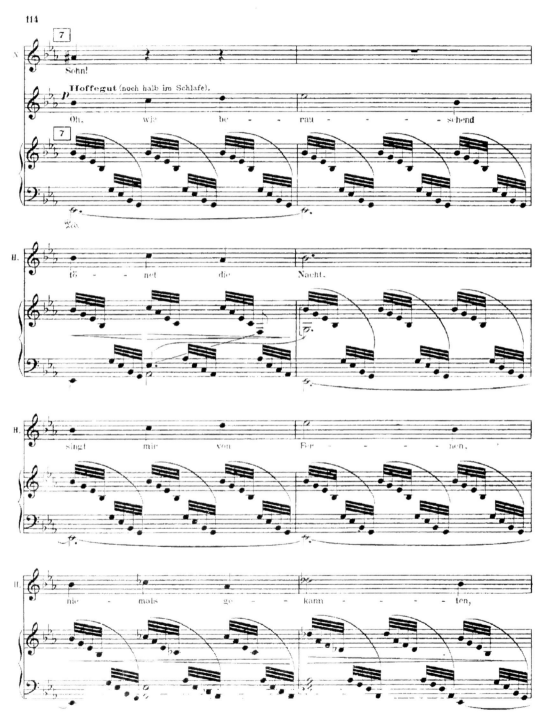

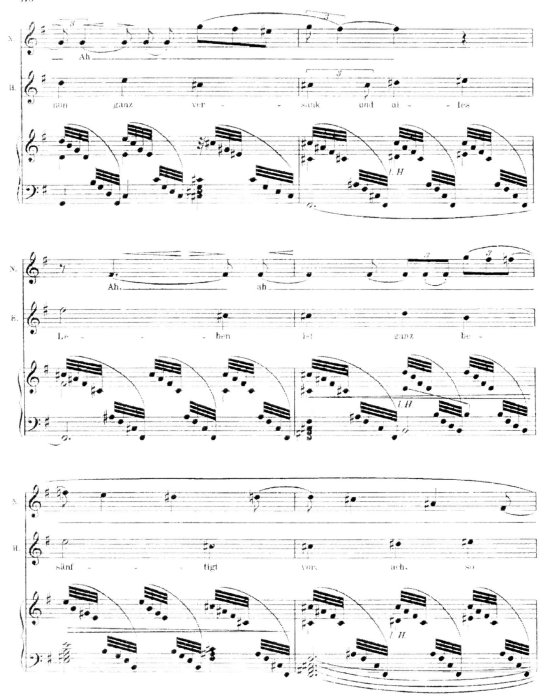

wenn zwi - schen dunk - len Bäu - men das

al - te Mär - chen schallt. Die Berg' im Mon-des-schim - mer

wie in Ge - dan - ken stehn und durch verworr-ne Träu - mer die Quel-len kla -

- gend gehn. Wal - des

11 (Hier beginnt der Wald immer stärker zu rauschen.)

Um ein Kleines fließender.

Lan - gen möcht' ich dich, fas - sen möcht' ich dich, dein sü - ßes
Stim - me-lein — da ich's nun ein - mal nicht kann in — mich sau - gen,
e - wig-lich, e - wig-lich warm — um mich ha - ben,
na - he ganz na - he, ganz na - he um mich ha - ben e - wig -

126

Allmählich ruhiger werdend.

zögernd

Nachtigall. [27] Noch verbreiternd.

[27] Noch verbreiternd.

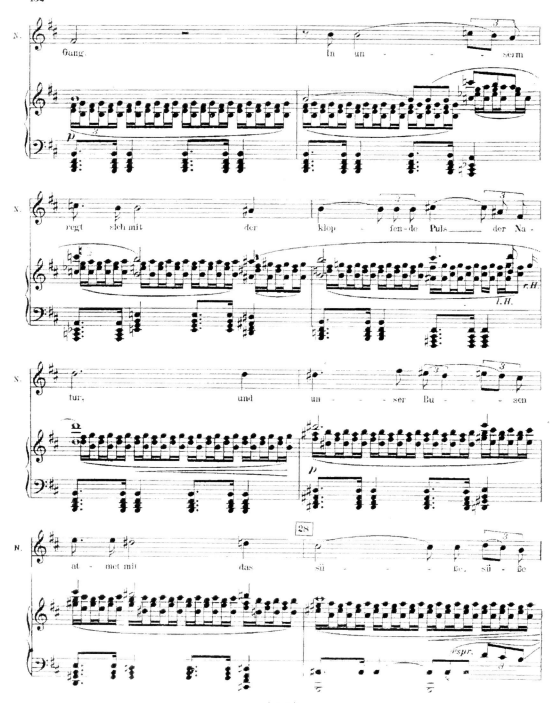

134

185

136

Ach,___ hol - de Nach-ti-gall, das ist Lie - - -

be, Lie - be zu dir, die___ mich er - hebt,

hell - se - hend mich macht, wie dich!___

(In diesem Augenblick ist das Bühnenbild ganz verändert. Alle Bäume erscheinen im Mon-
de wie transparent, die Blumen erglühn, alles ist von einem zittrigen Lichte erfüllt. Quellen
und Bäume rauschen stärker, auch sieht man viele Nachtfalter und Glühwürmer.)

(Leichter Wind; Gräser und Blumen zittern.)

Ah, _____ ah, ah, ah! _____

uns _ _ re Düf _ _ te!

Glockenspiel.

l. H.

41

Hoffegut.

Ach, _____ was ist mit mir?   Dies ist dei _ _ ne Stim _ me und

Ah!

Wer   uns   flie _ _ _ het,

41

42

Allmählich drängender.

42

Allmählich drängender.

44 Das Zeitmaß ist nun erheblich bewegter geworden.

44 Das Zeitmaß ist nun erheblich bewegter geworden.

45 Hoffegut.

148

51 Etwas fließender.

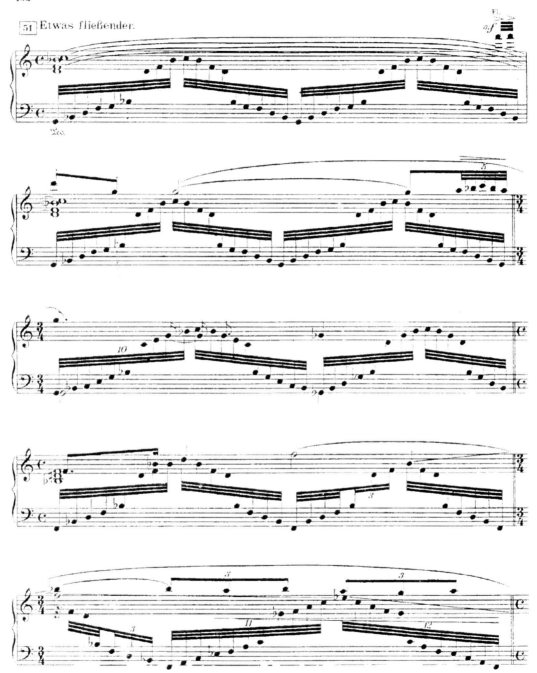

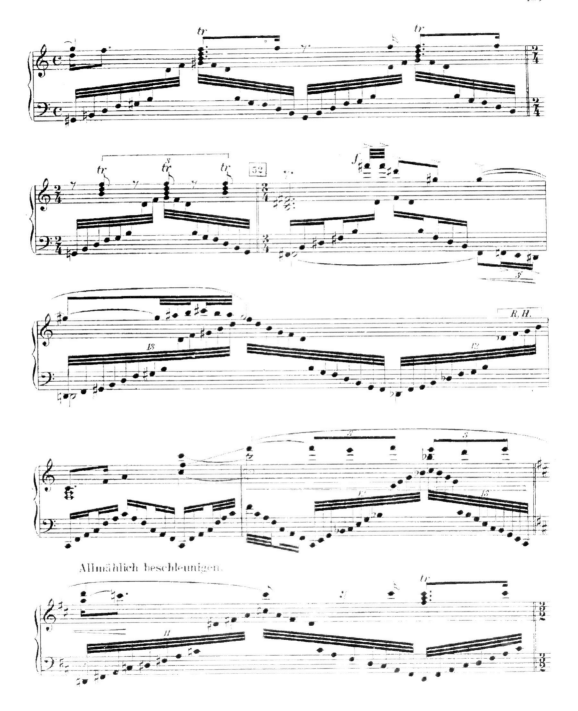

Allmählich beschleunigen.

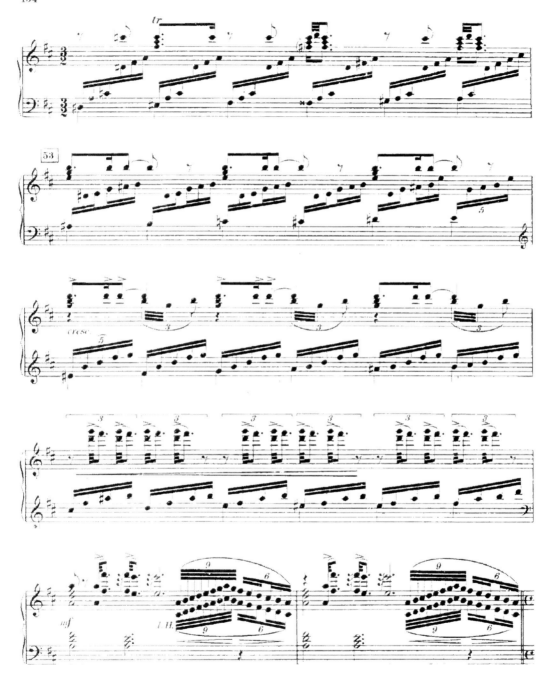

Die Sonne bestrahlt nun die in der Luft sichtbar gewordene „Stadt" welche sich einer Fata morgana gleichend, über den Horizont zieht. Der Chor der Vögel, von Wiedhopf und Ratefreund geführt, strömt auf die Szene.

R. könnt ihr Vög - lein euch freun, weil ihr jetz - und Kö - ni - ge seid.

59

R. Denn al - les was lebt,__ sei es

CHOR.

Sopr. (jubelnd)
Kön' - ge sind wir, Her - ren sind wir!

Alt.
Kön' - ge sind wir, Her - ren sind wir!

Ten.
Kön' - ge sind wir, Her - ren sind wir!

Bass.
Kön' - ge sind wir, Her - ren sind wir!

59

R. Mensch o - der Tier,__ was em - sig sich re - get in Flur__ o - der Hain,

Tanz-Szene.

(Im Hintergrund der Bühne wird eine große Menge Vögel sichtbar. Zaunschlüpfer sucht die durcheinander Wimmelnden

zu ordnen; zunächst scheint es ihm nicht zu gelingen.)

62

sag. Zaunschlüpferchen, was du bringst, was so stolz die Brust dir bläht?

Gib Kun - de mir,

Ob.

p

Wieder sehr lebhaft.

gib Kun - de mir, sag an!

p

f

Gibt es gar ei - ne Hoch - zeit? Sind es zärt - li - che Brautleut, die hier als er - stes Paar der

p

p

Stadt sich nah'n? In fest - li - chem Rei - gen

U. E. 6420.

z. heu - ern: als er - stes Paar in die neu - e Stadt sollt_ ihr

z. al - le, sie fest - lich ge - lei - ten.

64 **Ruhig.**

CHOR.

Sopr.

Frau Tau - be soll_ er schei - nen, Frau

Alt.

Frau Tau - be kom - me, sie

64 **Ruhig.**

Tau - be ist_ will - kom - men, sie bring' uns ih - ren Lieb - sten, will -

ist will - kom - men, sie bring' uns ih - ren

(Vogel Straße kommen und kehren mit ihren Schweifen die Bühne.)

65 **Etwas lebhafter.**

(Pelikane als Polizisten drängen die neugierig vordringende Vogelschar zurück.)

Schneller. Tempo.   **Schneller.**

(Kraniche und andere große Vögel tragen auf Stangen ein fertiges Nest herbei, das zwei Eingänge hat

66 Etwas breiter.

und in der Mitte eine Art Fenster.)
Wieder belebend.

(Paradiesvögel und kleinere exotische Vogel schmücken das Nest mit Blumen und bunten Beeren.)

(Das Nest steht fertig da.) Zaunschlüpfer.

Nest ge-baut.

naht die Braut. Nest ge-baut, wie ihr schaut wohl - ge-baut, naht die Braut.

Sehr lebhaft.

(Es naht die Hochzeitsmusik. Die Musikanten sind größenteils sehr bunte Vögel,

realistischer gekleidet wie die übrigen, auch tragen sie Gesichtsmasken.)

Ruhig bewegt.

[Es naht die „Braut" eine rosa Taube, verschämt und gefühlvoll, ihre

Brautjungfern umgeben sie.]

(Der Täuberich ist nun ganz siegesbewußt.)

(Die Taube ist ganz hingegeben.)

178

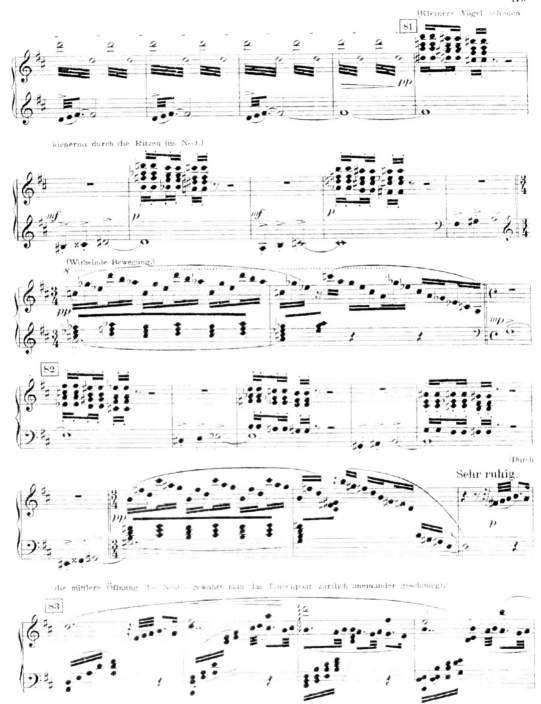

(Kleinere Vögel schauen

kienernd durch die Ritzen ins Nest.)

(Wirbelnde Bewegung.)

Sehr ruhig.

(Durch

die mittlere Öffnung des Nestes gewahrt man das Taubenpaar zärtlich aneinander geschmiegt.)

84

zögernd Lebhaft.

(Die ganze Vogelschar (Tänzer und Zuschauer) umkreist nun das Nest in

etwas beschleunigen

ausgelassenem Wirbel.)

Presto.

(Das Nest wird wieder auf Stangen gesteckt und, der neuen „Stadt" entgegen, fortgetragen.)

Einzelne Vögel (hinter der Szene).

Halt, halt!

Wiedhopf.

Was be-deu-tet dies?

Ch.
4.S.

Halt den Dieb, halt den Dieb!

[87]

(In höchster Aufregung kommen neue Vögel hereingestürzt.)

W.

Welch ein Auf-ruhr!

Chor.
Sopran.

So schnell als möglich.

Un - er-hör-stes Ge-scheh - nis, das

Sopran.

je - seit Vogel-gedenkengescheh'n!

Alt.

Unerhörtes Geschehnis, das je - seit Vogel-gedenken geschehen.

Langsam.

Prometheus. (mit etwas mehr Kraft.)

All-wo ich wei - le ist Mor-gen-nicht, nicht A - bend und nicht neb-Ech - te

pp

Wieder lebhafter.

Ratefreund.

Ver-däch-tig, Freund feind so, die scheinst du mir. gib mir Be - wei - se erst, daß wir dir dür - fen

Nacht.

Wieder lebhafter.

trau - en!

Breit.

piu f

Euch Men-schen einst war ich all - zu-sehr

mf

Breit.

l.H.

97 Noch gedehnter.

Freund; euch Vö - gel-völk - chen a - ber lieb' ich stets als der Gott-heit lieb - lich-stes

p espr.

ha - ben wir hier auf - ge-rich - tet, was die Gott - heit uns zu Dien - sten,

uns___ für ew' - ge Zei - ten al - le Men - schen zu Skla - ven

Breit.

macht. **Prometheus.**

Lieb seid ihr, das ist wahr; der Gott-heit Lä - cheln schuf euch die Ge-stalt, ihr,

Zwischenreich der sü - ßen Phan-ta-sie. Wo

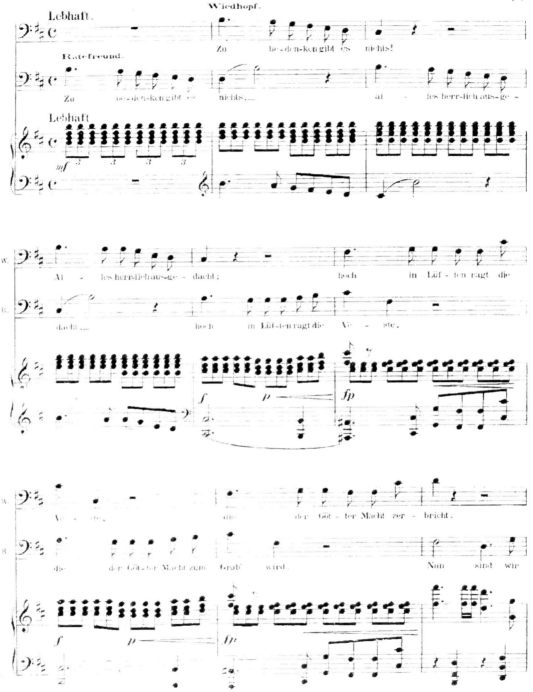

198

(Prometheus erhebt sich (ich erhebt sich und lüftet seinen Mantel ein wenig.)

203

Allmählich ein wenig fließender.

Fließend.

Gold - strah - len thro - - ne

sitzt er ge - wal - tig und

all' eu - er Trei - ben es

ist ihm ein Spiel.

U. b. u. a. o.

Wir wer - den uns zu weh - ren wis - sen,

Er kommt, er kommt zu stra-fen euch!

die Lo-sung ist ge-ge - ben, sie lau - tet: Krieg!

Sopr. (Jubelschrei!)
Krieg! Krieg!

Alt. (Jubelschrei!)
Krieg! Krieg!

Ten. (Jubelschrei!)
Krieg! Krieg!

Baß (Jubelschrei!)
Krieg! Krieg!

(Am Himmel hat sich schwarzes Gewölk gesammelt, das nur in der

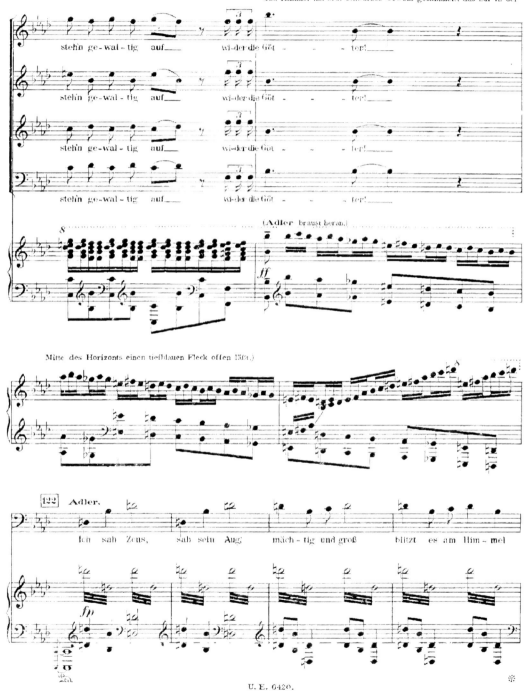

stehn ge-wal-tig auf__ wi-der die Göt _ _ ter!__

stehn ge-wal-tig auf__ wi-der die Göt _ _ ter!

stehn ge-wal-tig auf__ wi-der die Göt _ _ ter!

stehn ge-wal-tig auf__ wi-der die Göt _ _ ter!

(Adler braust heran.)

Mitte des Horizonts einen tiefblauen Fleck offen läßt.)

122 Adler.

Ich sah Zeus, sah sein Aug; mäch - tig und groß blitzt es am Him - mel

Wiedhopf.

Was denkst du nun _____ zu tun, o

Freund?

Ratefreund.

Be - setzt die Zin - nen, die To - re be-wacht,

hoch in Lüf - te die Seg - - - - ler!

126 Wiedhopf.

Chor der Vögel.

Sopran. 129

We - he, weh, es naht ein furcht-bar Un - ge - wit - ter, weh, nun stürzt der Him - mel ü - ber uns zu - sam - men, kein Er - bar - men, kein Er - bar - men

Ratefreund.

Ver - flucht - ter Re - gen das,

kennt der Him - mel, kennt der Him - mel mehr.

Stimmen der Winde.

Stimme des Zeus.

Stimme des Zeus.

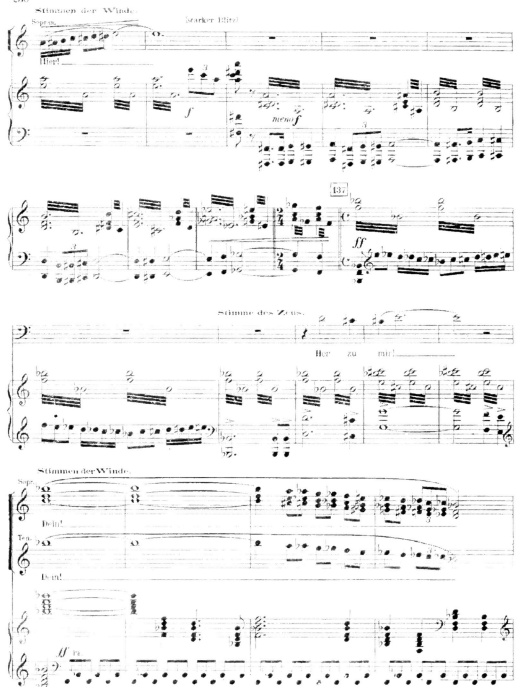

(Eine Wolkenerscheinung, einer riesigen Hand gleichend, greift über den Horizont und

138

packt das Nest an.)   Stimme des Zeus.   Dehnend.

Nhe - der!

Tempo.

(Ein starker Blitz schlägt ins Nest, das sogleich aufflammt. Teile stürzen brennend auf die Bühne.)

139

140 (Strömender Regen.)

Etwas mäßiger.
(Es hellt sich langsam auf. Einzelne Vögel kommen wieder zum Vorschein und zeigen sich in sichtlicher Weise von dem Natur-schauspiel ergriffen.)

141

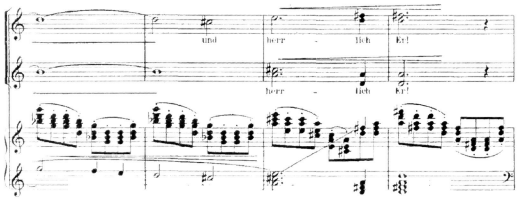

244

Bedeutend ruhiger.

248

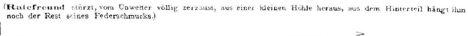

(**Ratefreund** stürzt, vom Unwetter völlig zerzaust, aus einer kleinen Höhle heraus, aus dem Hinterteil hängt ihm noch der Rest seines Federschmucks.)

Lebhaft.

Ratefreund.

Zum Kuk-kuk, Freund.

das war ein Spaß, wie bin ich pu - - - - del - naß! O, welch ein

Blöd-sinn, hie-her zu wan-deln, mit dem Wiedhopf an-zu-ban-deln, ei-ne Stadt gar auf

Wol - ken zu bau'n, o welch ein Grau'n, o welch ein Blöd - sinn! Dann das Ge-wit-ter,

Mir zit-tern al - le Glie - der, läuft das Was-ser zum Schuh hin-aus; ach,

hätt' ich das einz'-ge doch hier ge-lernt, das einz'-ge, was ich jetzt brau - chen könnt, das

Flie - - - - - - gen, das

(Indem er mit den kläglichen Resten seines Federschmucks vergeblich zu
flattern sich bemüht, trottet er ab.)

Flie - - - - gen!

253

So ist dies al - les denn ge-we - sen, wie? vor-bei,

ein Nichts, ein Traum, ge-träumt um zu ver-wehn.

Sehr ruhig.
Hoffegut.

Breit.
Klar.

stand ich ei - ne Stun-de, wie lauscht ich, wie lauscht ich

se - lig dei - ner Kun - de, wie sprachst du süß

poco f

Sehr ruhig.

was ich von eh ge-wußt, ge - wußt.

espr *dim.* *p espr.* *pp*

Wo ist dies nun? so ist es tot, ver-schlossen, un-er - öff-bar in der Brust?

p *pp*

während leichter Dunst die Bühne erfüllt, und ist schon halb verschwunden als plötzlich aus dem Gebüsch der

Ruf der Nachtigall ertönt, und man glaubt sie zu sehen.)

(Hoffegut bemüht sich sichtlich, den Sinn der Töne zu verstehn und bricht schließlich in Tränen aus. Sein Schluchzen

mühsam bekämpfend, entschwindet er talwärts.)

Vorhang.

OPERN, ORATORIEN U. CHORWERKE
IN KLAVIERAUSZÜGEN MIT TEXT

d. = deutsch, e. = englisch, f. = französisch, i. = italienisch, lat. = lateinisch

KLASSISCHE UND ÄLTERE WERKE

A. Opern

U.E.Nr.

3151 Adam Postillon von Lonjumeau (Kleinmichel) d.
3150 — Schweizerhütte (Kleinm.) d.
5141 Auber Fra Diavolo (Kleinm.) d.
3152 — Maurer u. Schlosser (do.) d.
678 Beethoven Egmont (Kienzl) d.
197 — Fidelio (Kienzl) d.
935 Bellini Norma (Kienzl) d. i.
3780 — Norma (Fd. Mottl) d.
3153 — Puritaner (Kleinmichel) d.
5140 Berlioz Fausts Verdammung (Volbach) d.
2788 Bizet G. Carmen mit der Ballett-Einlage (W. Kienzl) d.
3255 — Djamileh d.
3151 Boieldieu Neuer Gutsherr (Kleinmichel) d.
5355 — Rotkäppchen (Kleinm.) d.
725 — Weiße Dame (Heuberger) d.
3154 Dasselbe (Kleinmichel)
3156 Cherubini Portugiesischer Gasthof d.
3157 Wasserträger (Kleinm.) d.
3158 Cimarosa Die heimliche Ehe (do.) d.
3159 Dalayrac Die beiden Savoyarden (Kleinmichel) d.
3160 Ditersdorf Doktor u. Apotheker (Kleinmichel) d.
3161 — Hieronymus Knicker (do.) d.
754 Donizetti Lucia (Schalk) d.
915 — Regimentstochter (Schalk) d.
3206 — Dasselbe (Kleinmichel) d.
3162 Flotow Martha (Wüst) d.
4943 — Stradella (Wüst) d.
3143 Gluck E. trageuse Kadi (Fuchs) d.
3761 — Alceste (Fd. Mottl) d.
2685 — Iphigenie in Aulis. Nach Wagner richtig. (e. Bulow) d.
914 — Orpheus (Fischer) d. i.
2500 — Iphigenie auf Tauris (Strauss) d.
5161 65 Grétry Die beiden Geizigen, Richard Löwenherz (Kleinmichel) d.
728 Halévy Die Jüdin (F. Schalk) d.

4617 Haydn Der Apotheker d.
3156 Hérold Der Zweikampf d.
5157 Hiller Im Jagd (Kleinm.) d.
3168 65 Isouard Ste. Aschenbrödel, Lotterielos (Kleinmichel) d.
5209 Kreutzer Nachtlager in Granada (Kleinmichel) d.
755 — Dasselbe (Kienzl) d.
3170 — Verschwunden (Kleinm.) d.
5171 Lortzing Ali Pascha (Kruse) d.
5172 — Casanova (Kleinmichel) d.
3174 — Hans Sachs (Kleinm.) d.
3176 — Opernprobe (Kleinm.) d.
544 — Undine (Kienzl) d.
462 — Waffenschmied (Kienzl) d.
587 — Wildschütz (Kienzl) d.
469 — Zar und Zimmermann (Kienzl) d.
3768 Maillart Glöckchen des Eremiten d. f.
647 Marschner Hans Heiling (Kienzl) d.
5175 — Templer u Jüdin (Kleinm.) d.
3176 Méhul Schatzgräber (Kleinm.) d.
5177 — Joseph (Weingartner) d. f.
753 Mendelssohn Sommernachtstraum (Kienzl) d.
2977 Meyerbeer Afrikanerin d. f.
3195 — Hugenotten (Kogel) d.
2457 — Prophet (Kogel) d.
5179 — Robert der Teufel Kleinm. d.
5179 Monsigny Der Deserteur (Kleinmichel) d.
5180 Mozart Bastien und Bastienne d.
2556 — Cosi fan tutte (Levi) d. i.
270 — Don Juan (mit Secco-Rezit.) (Kienzl) d. i.
3187 — Entführung aus dem Serail (Kleinmichel) d.
3191 — Figaros Hochzeit d.
117 — Hochzeit des Figaro (Brüll) d.
917 — Idomeneo (Horn) d. i.
916 — Zauberflöte (Kienzl) d. i.
3149 Müller W. Die Schwestern von Prag (Kleinmichel) d.
733 Nicolai Lustige Weiber von Windsor d.

3184 85 Paër Kapellmeister, Lustige Schuster (Kleinmichel) d.
3186 Paisiello Schöne Müllerinde d.
3187 Pergolese La Maid als Herrn (Kleinmichel) d.
193 Rossini Barbier (Brüll) d. i.
3207 — Dasselbe (Kleinmichel) d.
3168 — Tancred (Kleinmichel) d.
5149 — Tell (Kleinmichel) d.
3189 Rubinstein Die sibirischen Jäger (Kleinmichel) d.
771 Rückauf Rosenstein d.
3190 Schenk Der Dorfbarbier (Kleinmichel) d.
3191 Schubert Der häusliche Krieg (Die Verschworenen) d.
5702 — Gefesselte Phantasie (Mottl) d.
5702 Wagner Rich. Rienzi (Klindworth) d.
5931 — (Singer) d. e.
5901 — Holländer (Klindworth) d.
5935 — (Singer) d. e.
5906 — Tannhäuser (Klindworth) d.
5935 — (Singer) d. e.
5847 — (Pariser Bearbeitung) d. e.
5908 — Lohengrin (Klindworth) d.
5937 — (Singer) d. e.
5902 — Lohengrin (erleichtert)
1725 — Tristan (Bülow) d.
5910 — (Klindworth) d.
5057 — (Singer) d. e.
5907 — Meistersinger (Klindw.) d. e.
5941 — (Singer) d. e.
5911 — Rheingold (Klindworth) d.
5943 — (Singer) d. e.
5916 — Walküre (Klindworth) d.
5945 — (Singer) d. e.
5919 — Siegfried (Klindworth) d.
5047 — (Singer) d. e.
5920 — Götterdämmerung (Klindworth) d.
5048 — (Singer) d. e.
5931 — Parsifal (Klindworth) d.
5051 — (Singer) d. e. Arrangement von Kogel
5872 — Rienzi d.
5873 — Holländer d.
5874 — Tannhäuser d.
192 Weber Abu Hassan (Kleinm.) d. i.
2847 — Euryanthe (Rössler) d.

471 Weber Freischütz (Kienzl) d.
726 — Oberon (Kienzl) m. allen Rez. d.
5737 — Preciosa (Rössler) d.
5231 Wolf Das zerbrochene Opferfest (Kleinmichel) d.

B. Oratorien (Chorwerke etc.)

5041 Bach J. S. Johannes-Passion (Kehlhoffer) d.
840 — Matthäus-Passion (Vockner)
853 — Messe H moll (Vockner) lat.
108 Beethoven Missa solemnis (Kienzl) lat
2539 Berlioz op. 5 Requiem (Gr Totenmesse) (Ph. Scharwenka) d.
5047 Gluck Musenhöhngun (Fuchs-Kallbeck)
721 Händel Messias (Reiter) d. e.
1746 — Israel d. e.
1743 — Josua d. e.
1644 — Judas Macca-bäus d. e.
1657 — Samson d. e.
4551 Sauli d. e.
480 Haydn Jahreszeiten (Heuberger) d.
4940 — Schöpfung (Heuberger) d. e.
4930 — Tobias Heimkehr (Glosser) d.
561 — Die 7 Worte des Erlösers am Kreuz (Ed. Kremser) d.
1788 Liszt Die heilige Elisabeth d. e.
4787 Mendelssohn Elias (J. V. Woss) d. e.
821 — Paulus (Heuberger) d. e.
480 — Walpurgisnacht (Orel) d.
7580 Mozart Krönungsmesse C dur lat.
589 — Requiem (R. Hirschfeld) lat
205 Pergolese Stabat mater lat
2481 Rossini Das Lied von der Glocke d.
2585 Schubert Messe in Es (Spengel) lat
1730 Wagner Liebesmahl der Apostel

NEUERE MODERNE WERKE

A. Opern

5771 Bittner J. Das höllisch Gold d.
5713 — Der liebe Augustin d.
3756 — Bergsee d.
6316 — Abenteurer d.
6130 — Die Kohlhaymerin d.
6135 — Todesarmschild d.
6145 Braunfels Prinzessin d.
6420 Braunfels op. 30 Die Vögel d.
1754 Cornelius Barbier von Bagdad (Levi-Mottl) d.
2794 — Dasselbe (Mottl) d.
1375 — Der Cid (Thuille) Original-Ausgabe d.
6302 Delius Romeo u. Julia a. d. Dorfe (Junior) d.
6305 — Fennimore u. Gerda d.
6300 — Dasselbe englische Ausgabe e.
1300 Foerster J. B. Jessika d.
5501 — Dasselbe (tschechisch)
5810 — Maria-Eva d.
4617 — Übermacht (Nepřemožení) d. i. tschechisch
6250 Gál H. Arzt der Sobeïde d.
5640 Goetz Der Widerspenstigen Zähmung d.
727 Goldmark Heimchen am Herd d.
3956 — Die Königin v. Saba d.
3560 Goldschmidt A. v. Gaea (Cyr. Hynais) d.
3705 Graener Das Narrengericht d.
5576 — Don Juanoletzt Abenteuer d.
5965 — Theophano d.
5336 Hubay Geigenmacher von Cremona d.
4951 — Moor-rochara d.
5471 Janáček Jenufa d. tsch.
5185 — Broucek tsch.

5285 Klenau P. v. Sulamith d.
5971 — Kjartan u Gudrun d.
5664 Lia Hans Maria v. Magdala d.
5971 Mahler-Weber Oberon d.
7553 Maxwell J. Mascot d.
6416 Raucke W. Laurin Rosengarten d.
5770 — Fest des Lebens d.
5931 Krenek Belar d.
6270 Koetisal Meister Guido d.
5395 Novák Vit. op. 49 Zvikovsky rarách (Sarakobold) (sch.)
5416 — Karlstein tsch.
6190 Offenbach Goldschmied von Toledo d.
6125 Rezniček Ritter Blaubart d.
6951 Schillings Mona Lisa d.
5090 Schreker Fr. Der ferne Klang (Berg) d.
5770 — Das Spielwerk (Knabl) d.
5690 — Die Gezeichneten (Gmeindl) d.
6136 — Der Schatzgräber d.
6130 Schuster Jungbrunnen d.
6295 Sicardi Herr Dandolo d.
607 Smetana Das Geheimnis d.
409, 411 — Der Kuß (Balfser) d.
5609 — Die verkaufte Braut d.
5597 Smyth E. Der gute Freund (The Boatswain's Mate) d. e.
6516 — Strandrecht (The Wreckers) d.
6115 Štěpán Lied d.
1682 Strauss R. op. 25 Guntram (O. Singer) d.
4185 Stradiot Der türkisenblaue Garten d.
5912 Szymanowski op. 45 Hagith d. poln.
7057 Tschaikowsky Eugen Onegin d.

5195 Ulmer op. 73 Rhapsodie d.
5977 Weingartner op. 51 Kain und Abel d.
5695 — op. 57 Dame Kobold d.
5220 — op. 54 Die Dorfschule d.
5177 — op. 65 Der Sturm d.
5715 — op. 66 Meister Andrea d.
6135 Wellesz E. Die Prinzessin Girnara d.
6030 Winternitz Meister Oroban d.
6475 Zajerek-Blackeman Jung Helmbrecht d.
6450 — Ferdinand und Luise d.
6603 Zemlinsky op. 15 Florentinische Tragödie d.
6630 — Der Zwerg d.

B. Oratorien (Chorwerke etc.)

1750 Brahms op. 53 Rhapsodie d.
6676 Braunfels Die Ammenuhr d.
422 Bruckner Te Deum (J. Schalk)
2987 — Dasselbe und Symphonie IX zusammen
9915 — Messe II E moll Orgelauszug lat
5901 — Messe III (Gross) F moll lat.
7705 — Helgoland (Hynais) d.
5927 — 150. Psalm d.
5900 Delius Appalachia (Singer) d. e.
5955 — Eine Arabeske d. e.
5896 — Im Meerestreiben (S. Fall) d. e.
5906 — Messe des Lebens (Singer) d.
6571 — Requiem d. e.
6918 — Sonnenuntergangslieder d. e.
7057 Tschaikowsky op. 56 Stabat Material

1125 Orelth op. 14 Jung Rukens (4 Bände) d.
6954 Klenau Cornel Bilke d.
8115 Klose Der Sonne Geist d.
1651 Mahler Das klagende Lied (Wöss) d.
5650 — VIII. Symphonie (Wöss) fol. d.
3821 — Das Lied von der Erde (Wöss) d.
5896 Marx Herbstchor an Pan d.
5235 — Morgengesang d. e.
5067 Mittmann op. 107 Kriegsmesse d.
5372 Müller-Hermann op 27 Symphonie d.
3357 Novák VII. op. 43 Sturm d. tsch.
5293 — op. 18 Totenbraut (Vesely) tsch.
1436 Reger op. 21 Hymne d.
3481 — op. 114 Die Nonnen d.
5430 — op. 130 Römischer Triumphgesang d.
5340 Reznicek In Memoriam d.
5696 Schönberg Gurre-Lieder (Berg)
5696 — Dasselbe Büttenausgabe
3877 Schreker op. 11 Schwanengesang d.
5495 Smyth Ethel Nacht d. e.
6193 Springer Max Königslied d.
5911 — Abend auf Golgatha (Orgel-Partitur) d.
1437 Strauss R. op. 14 Wanderers Sturmlied d.
5483 Vaniček Jan Hus tsch.
2820 Wöss Heiliges Lied (Gand) d.
1871 Wolf Hugo Christnacht d.
5861 Zemlinsky Alex. Der 83 Psalm d.

Bei Bestellungen genügt die Angabe der jedem Werke vorgedruckten Nummer. — In ordering kindly mention Universal-Edition and number only. Pour les commandes il suffit d'indiquer le numéro de l'oeuvre.

UNIVERSAL-EDITION A. G. WIEN-NEW YORK

CPSIA information can be obtained at www.ICGtesting.com
Printed in the USA
BVOW02s1008190315

392427BV00013B/130/P